CW00433725

GOODE
POLAND

Growing up.
Deportation and
Internment in Siberia.
The war years.

The Memoirs of Stefan
Bogusław Mączka

Whilst every effort has been made to remain faithful to historical records, this isn't a history book. The memoirs are based on the recollections of the author.

A CIP catalogue record for this title is available from the British Library

Printed in the United Kingdom

First Published January 2013

ISBN 978-0-9571312-4-8 Paperback Edition

Also available on Kindle.

Published by: www.skinnybirdproductions.com

Front cover: Stefan Maczka with sister Danuta and friend, Irena Czarnecka in Palestine 1943

CONTENTS

Foreword

Introduction

1   My father

2   My young days at Osada

3   War and deportation to Siberia

4   Life and work in Siberia

5   Escape from Siberia, 14th November 1941

6   Military training in the Middle East

7   Italy: Monte Cassino

8   Adriatic Campaign

9   After the war

The Author

Obituary

Postscript

Further Reading

FOREWORD

My father was a strong man.
Proud. Indomitable. Like so many of his countrymen. On February 10th, 1940, he and his family suffered a great injustice. They were forced out of their home by Soviet officials into sledges, and hauled across the snow in temperatures unbelievably cold, and deported to Siberia by train, on a cattle-truck, a hellish journey that took days before they arrived in a work camp. The beginning of a living nightmare. Treated as little more than slaves, worked hard, starved and freezing in the bitter cold, they weren't the only ones to suffer.

In four mass deportations, approximately 1.7 million Poles were uprooted from their homes, and the land they knew and loved. Each has their story. Goodbye Poland is my father's.

Two days before he died, we spoke, he and I. 'How's the book going?' I asked.
'I'm too busy for the book,' he said. He went on to explain that he had a meeting in London, a Polish war veterans march on Remembrance Sunday, a television interview lined up, a meeting which Prince Charles was expected to attend, all these things to prepare for, and which he was looking forward to.
He didn't make it. He died on 5 November 2014, aged ninety-one.

As I read his book for the third time, it occurred to me that maybe he'd lived such a long life, despite his ordeal, because he had a job to do, to help ensure future generations don't forget what he and his fellow Poles went through, that their contribution to our freedom would be recognised and remembered.

What follows is his story, in his own words. His voice, his accent preserved - he wrote exactly as he spoke - and therefore not always grammatically correct, but for those who knew and loved him, that voice, is instantly recognizable.

This foreword is dedicated to: All victims of oppression. And survivors. Everywhere.

Brian Maczka

INTRODUCTION

I am writing this book for the benefit of my four children, seven grandchildren, currently three great-granddaughters, and a great-grandson. To let them know about my Polish background, how and why I came to this country in 1946, and still speak with a foreign accent.

Second influence to write my memoirs was Geoffrey Giddings MC a great friend since 1957, in business, a director at Kind & Co, and in the Leytonstone Rotary Club.

Geoff found a considerable gap in his father's life; he only knew that he worked in the city, because he wore a business suit with bowler hat, and carried a briefcase and rolled up umbrella, but he had no idea what was his job. So, he decided to write his memoirs in order that his children and grandchildren would know about his part in 1939-1945 war. The third reason, was that on meeting number of sons of Polish war veterans they had no idea about their father's war effort, other than they fought at Monte Cassino. I started writing at the age of 81in 2003, some friends were surprised that I can remember anything after such a long time.

On leaving the Soviet Union in April 1942 Poles were warned by NKVD (KGB) not to speak about our time in USSR. Many Poles, including my sister Danuta, would not talk, being afraid of the long arm of NKVD, others just wanted to forget about this Hell on Earth, this cruel and inhuman country of USSR. The ordinary citizens of Soviet Union were also the victims of this brutal regime of Stalin.

At first I also would not talk (I was not afraid of the NKVD), I was just trying to forget my traumatic and nightmarish experiences and to get on with my new life in this country, but I could not forget, most of it is indelibly imprinted in my mind. All the important events are so clear in my memory as if it all happened yesterday.

When I first talked to my English friends, they could not believe that USSR, our war allies, were capable of atrocities, such as Stalin's Ethnic Cleansing of 1.7 million Polish middle classes, kulaks. Murder of 15,000 Polish Officers in Katyn, murder of 4,500 Polish Policemen at Mednoje.

This British disbelief made me more determined to talk about my experiences in the Soviet Union. In 1974, I was asked by my Rotary Club to give a talk about my Siberian experiences. My club members found it very interesting and I was invited to speak to other Rotary Clubs. One member of my club, being owner of the local newspaper, wrote an article about me. This followed during the next 38 years, by talks to other clubs, Round Tables, Women's Leagues and many others.

10th of March 2005, I gave a talk about my experiences covering period from Sep 1939, to the end of the War in 1945, to the 2nd year students of History at East Anglia University in Norwich.

One of the students asked me, who was the worst, Hitler or Stalin?

I replied, both were very bad, the only difference is that Stalin had more time before and after the war to kill millions more, including his own citizens.

I received the following letters from UEA Norwich:

First dated 17 March 2005

Dear Mr Maczka

I am returning the copy of your memoirs which I have read with great interest. I also want to thank you again for speaking to our students. I know they got a lot out of it: several have told me so. It is a pity that the computer projection did not work properly but it was much more valuable to hear of your experiences. This was a vivid and real account and, as the students told me, much better than a dry academic board.

Please accept my thanks again. We have in the School of History a mini-library and I shall deposit the copy of Stalin's Ethnic Cleansing there so that it is available to all.

With best wishes

Yours sincerely,

Roger Munting

Second letter dated 28 April 2005

Dear Mr Maczka

Excuse my writing to you again but I wanted you to know this.

As you may know, at the end of each semester we circulate a questionnaire to students to gain feedback about the course they have just taken. On this occasion several students made favourable comments about your talk. I should add that they were all unprompted and anonymous. One wrote: 'I really enjoyed having the guest speaker. He was a remarkable and interesting man. Is there any chance he will return to UEA?'

In my experience students do not make such comments lightly. This underlines how much we appreciate the trouble you took in talking to our students.

With best wishes

Yours sincerely,

Roger Munting

Most frequent question was, "Why don't you write a book?"

I always replied; "I am too busy at my job, but I will try to write when I retire." Realizing that at 81, (so far in excellent health), the time is not on my side, I decided to make a start, and eight years later, I am still writing, rather on and off, not consistently. I am not a writer and I don't try to pretend that I can write. I find it difficult to express myself correctly in writing. So, I decided to write my story like a Business Report in chronological date order of events.

After invasion of Poland on 17 September 1939, Stalin started his policy of ethnic cleansing of middle classes from Eastern Poland. By deporting about 1.7 millions Polish citizens to Siberia, it is impossible to verify the actual figures, which vary between various sources, from 1.2 to 1.7 millions of which about 50% perished in the Soviet Union (large numbers remained, not being able to get out). The lack of accuracy should not distract us from the tragedy of the enormous numbers involved. I was lucky to come out alive and to be able to tell my story. In spite of a number of dangerous setbacks, and great difficulties in my life, I consider myself extremely lucky to have survived with good health, not affected mentally or physically.

I know that hundreds of thousands of my countrymen, women and children, had far worse experiences than mine. The extraordinary events that happened to me were not under my control, I was just swept away, like on an enormous wave.

Only three times I made decisions that could have changed my fate.

1st. I could have stayed behind after my escape from the wagon in Równe 12th February 1940, but I don't know what would have happened to me after that.

2nd. I volunteered to explore Railway Station in Kotlas.

3rd. My escape from Siberia with six friends, on 14th November 1941.

In writing about my experiences, I didn't try to make myself a hero; I made sure that my part was not exaggerated.

I hope that my grandchildren and great-grandchildren will be inspired by my story. What I came through and achieved in my life was by great determination, study, and very hard work, with large degree of good luck. I am grateful to my commanding officers who were pushing me on, by giving me difficult tasks to perform, if I protested I was told that everything is possible if you set your mind to it, just get on with it and do it. At that time, I thought that they were just picking on me, not realising that they may have seen a potential in me.

Only later on in my working life, I realised how much the army service was useful for me. Whenever I came across a difficult task, I would say to myself, "Stefan if you managed to survive Siberia, the war and very demanding Commanding Officers, then everything is possible."

In fact, it worked for me. I started to work in England as hotel porter (not knowing the English language), later on studying accountancy.

Ending my working life as Group Financial Director/Secretary of a Group of Construction Companies, and Managing Director of some of the subsidiaries.

To help to illustrate my narrative, I used a number of sources for photographs and maps:- from General Anders' book; Without Last Chapter, my sister Danuta's diary, my father's diary, Regimental books, Encyclopedia, maps from World Atlas and Internet. The photos from civilian life are mostly mine.

Very brief history of Poland

The origins of the Polish State are shrouded in obscurity due to the absence of written documents. However, the oral tradition of the Piast dynasty, which ruled the Polish Kingdom for over five hundred years, relates how Piast established his principality; at the start of the 9th century A.D. over the largest Polish tribes Polanie. By the time Piast great-great grandson Mieszko I was baptized in 966 and converted the whole country to Christianity, the Polish state comprised almost all various Polish tribes. The first crowned King of Poland was Boleslaw Chrobry the son on Mieszko I. In 1241, Poland suffered the most disastrous Mongol invasion. The southern part of the country was ravaged and most of the towns, including the capital Cracov were raised. The repeated raids by the Mongolian Tartars from Crimea continued until 17th century, only to be replaced by not less ferocious invasion of the Turks from the Ottoman Empire. One of the most eventful acts in Polish history was the treaty signed in 1385 at Krzew by the envoys of the Polish queen Saint Jadwiga and Jagiełło, the grand duke of Lithuania, the last pagan state in Europe. Early next year, Jagiełło was baptized in Cracov, married Saint Jadwiga, and was crowned king of Poland. He started a rapid conversion of Lithuania to Christianity. This personal union established Jagiellons as rulers of the largest realm in Christendom and started the Golden AGE in Polish history. The last king of the Jagiellons dynasty Zygmunt August convened in 1569 a meeting of Polish and Lithuanian parliament at Lublin, which agreed to transform the personal union of the two states into the Polish Lithuanian Rzeczpospolita (Commonwealth).

From 12th Century, Poland defended its borders successfully against hostile Turkish neighbour, until final defeat of Turkey, at the siege of Vienna in 1683, by King Jan Sobieski.

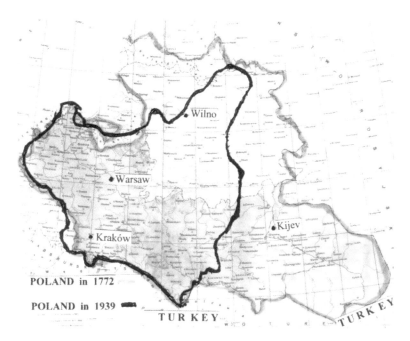

POLAND in 1772

POLAND in 1939

In 1772 Poland was the biggest country in Europe, with borders from Baltic to Black Sea

The XVIII century saw the inexorable decline of Rzeczpospolita and at the same time the enormous increase in power of its neighbours Austria, Prussia and Russia. These three Powers connived to destroy Poland and eventually agreed to divide between them the Polish territory. The first partition took place in 1772, the second in 1793.

In 1794, Kosciuszko uprising against Russia lasted from 28 March to 16 November 1794, finally defeated by Russia with the Prussian help.

The third partition in 1795, erased the Rzeczpospolita from the map of Europe. Polish population was subjected to slavery and forcible Germanisation and Russification.

The Polish nation revolted number of times against Russian and Prussian oppression, (Austrians were more liberal).

November uprising in Warsaw against Russia 29 November 1830 to October 1831.

January uprising against Russia, 22 January 1863, until October1864, covered kingdom of Poland, Lithuania, Byelorussia and part of Ukraine.

After 123 years, in 1918, Poland together with Baltic States, regained freedom and independence.

For further information: refer to History of Poland.

Stefan Mączka

October 2014.

CHAPTER ONE

MY FATHER

My father, Stefan Mączka, was born 25 October 1895, in Korytków, County of Radom, about 30 miles from Starachowice, Poland. His parents, Antoni and Salomea (nee Charazińska), had six sons and one daughter. Most of the Mączka family lived in Starachowice and Skarzysko-Kamienna, near Kielce, situated about 120 miles south of Warsaw. My father volunteered in 1918 for service in the Polish Army.

The Red Army invaded Poland in July 1920, with the aim of conquering whole of Europe.

General Mikhayl Tukhachevsky the commander of the Soviet Army, on 2nd July 1920, in Smolensk issued his order of the day:

"Soldiers of the Red Army, the time of reckoning has come. The army of the Red Banner and the predatory White Eagle face each other in mortal combat. Over the dead body of White Poland, shines the road to worldwide conflagration. On our bayonets, we shall bring happiness and peace to toiling humanity. To the West, the hour of attack has struck. On to Vilna, Minsk and Warsaw. March."

BALTIC SEA
LITUANIA
PRUSIA
WILNO
Danzig
GERMANY
GRODNO
Białystok
POZNAŃ
WARSZAWA
BRZEŚĆ
USSR
ŁÓDŹ
Starachowice
ROWNE
LUBLIN
KRAKÓW
LWÓW
CZECHOSLOVAKIA
1920 CURZON Line in Black

Poland's appeal to France and England for help and arms was refused. Poland was advised to negotiate for peace.

Soviets were now approaching Warsaw having already occupied eastern Poland. Lord Curzon, the British Foreign Minister, worried that Soviets would overrun the whole of Europe, tried to negotiate Armistice, by offering to Russia the Polish land that they had already occupied, on the condition that they stop further advance. Russians and Poles have rejected this offer. Lord Curzon's proposal for border between Poland and USSR had become known in diplomacy as a Curzon Line.

Jósef Pilsudski, the commander of Polish armed forces, appealed to the citizens for volunteers to join the Polish army to fight the invaders.

The Polish army, after regrouping, attacked on 15th August 1920, and defeated larger Soviet forces led by General M. Tukhachevsky. Please note that Stalin served in the invading Soviet Red Army.

This day is now remembered in Poland as Cud nad Wisla, Miracle of the Vistula.

The final victory over Red Army was on 30th August 1920, at Komarovo. It was the last big Polish cavalry battle of this century, successfully defeating the General Budionny's cavalry.

My father took part in this battle with his Krechowiecki cavalry regiment.

Stalin never forgot this humiliating defeat.

The Military Settlements (Osada's)

Polish Parliament by the Act dated 17 December 1920, granted plots of land along the eastern border with Russia, to 9000 soldiers as a reward for defeating Russians on the 30 August 1920. The ex-soldiers, now farmers, were armed and expected to be at battle readiness at all times. Until border guards were set-up in 1924, the military settlers, now Osadniks, had to defend the eastern borders against invading armed bands from Russia. In our area, the neighbouring villages were inhabited mainly by Ukrainian's, who in 1931, represented 68% of the whole population of the County of Wolyn. The towns on the other hand, were dominated by the Jewish population.

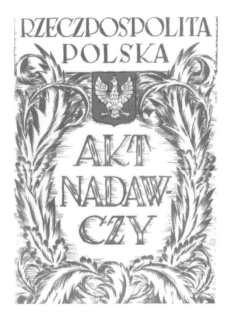 

Deed of Grant of Land by Polish Parliament to Stefan Maczka

My father Stefan Mączka a sergeant in the 1st Krechowiecki Lancers Regiment, received land with 96 other lancers at a settlement named after their regiment Osada Krechowiecka situated 20 miles from the Soviet borders.

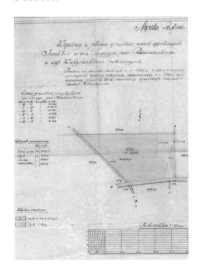

The surveyor's plan of my father's plot of land

12.5352 Hectares = 30.97 Acres.

My father's land marked pink on the map below, was situated at the cross roads from Równe in the west to Tuczyn in the East, Koźlin in the North to Horyngród in the South.

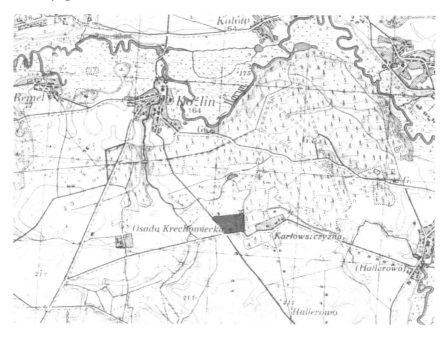

Map of Settlers Osada Krechowiecka 1922-1939

On adjoining land, further parcels of land had been allocated to ex soldiers of three other regiments, Osada Hallerowo, 52 plots, Osada Jazłowiecka, 10 plots, and Osada Bojanówka, 38 plots, forming the largest group of 169 military settlers in Eastern Poland.

The whole area given to the settlers, was mainly an ex Russian army training ground, criss-crossed by trenches, covered by artillery shells and other debris. But the soil was black and fertile.

The life on this land was very difficult, until settlers built their own houses; they lived mostly with local villagers. Not surprisingly, most of the men like my father, married local girls. Majority of the settlers had no farming experience. They had to start from nothing; helping one another to build houses, stables and barns, and to cultivate each others land. The comradeship forged in the army, continued on this settlement. Their regiment helped them financially only for the first 6 months.

Numbered plots of land allocated to Osadniks

S **School**
+ **Church**
OZ **Health Centre** as at 1939

Names of Settlers (Osadniks), with numbers of plots of land allocated as previous plan for plot numbers

1	Roman Cybulski
2	Zygmunt Górecki
3 wachm.	M. Kazimierz Weseliński
4 st. wachm.	Franciszek Głaszczka
5 st. wachm.	Józef Stobniak
6	Antoni Szymański
7 wachm.	Franciszek Biedul
8	Walenty Struzik
9	Józef Dobaj
10 plut.	Władysław Zieliński
11 ppor.	Bolesław Podhorski
12 uł.	Władysław Dąbrowski
13	Jan Dzierzgowski
14	Stefan Talarowski
15 wachm.	Włodzimierz Kulikowski
16 wachm.	Władysław Jakubowski
17 wachm.	Henryk Duszyński
18	Piotr Frączak
19	Ignacy Urbański
20 uł.	Wincenty Cała
21 plut.	Aleksander Chlewiński
22 plut.	Stefan Mączka
23 plut.	Szczepan Balmas
24 uł.	Zygmunt Jaruga
25 wachm.	Marcin Stępień
26 rtm.	Józef Płużański
27	Antoni Stasior (Sulimirski Józef)
43 mjr	Edward Milewski
44	Jakub Chromik
45	Feliks Bojankiewicz
46 wachm.	Władysław Gorzkowski
47 plut.	Gustaw Chanecki
48 kpr.	Franciszek Górczak
49 st. uł.	Franciszek Gałka
50 plut.	Józef Brzostowski
51 uł.	Franciszek Sterna
52 uł.	Stanisław Graniczny
53 wachm.	Jan Szymański
54 por.	Edward Czajkowski
55 wachm.	Piotr Swojnóg
56 uł.	Walery Radomski
57 st. wachm.	Stanisław Armatys
58 st. uł.	Antoni Kulik
59 uł.	Stanisław Wojna
60 uł.	Karol Kałusiewicz
61	Władysław Szymanik
62 uł.	Wojciech Morozowicz
63 uł.	Stefan Prochera
64	Józef Zwoliński
65	Romuald Graniczny
66	Józef Ogonowski
67	Wojciech Żygadło
68	Józef Wrzyszcz
69	Adolf Zajdel
70	Józef Szopa
71 uł.	Bronisław Kucharewicz
72	Zygmunt Wałasiewicz
73	Jan Zdanek
74 uł.	Modest Łoś
75 uł.	Władysław Paszyński
76	Jan Madej
77	Bernard Bujnowski
78	Kazimierz Kaczmarski
86	Jan Jankowski
87	Stefan Świerczyński
88 st. wachm.	Józef Mańka
89	Stefan Dobrzański
90 st. wachm.	Klemens Grzybowski
91	Wincenty Rzońca
92	Stanisław Boryń
93 plut.	Stanisław Pukacz
94	Aleksander Międza
95	Romuald Balicki
96 wachm.	Józef Kwiatek
97	Mieczysław Netwinko

Father in 1937, on his Arab horse called 'Siwy' (Grey)

Father on the left, sharpening his saw for cutting down trees to build his house with the help of his neighbours, Balmas and Cala

26th February 1922, Father at 26 years of age married a 19-year-old local girl from Tuczyn, Stanislawa Poznanska

They had 3 children:

Stefan Boguslaw 31/12/1922

Danuta Alexandra 21/03/1925

Zofia Leonarda 1/08/1926

My mother died 23 January 1928, buried at cemetery in Horyngród.

Each farm had to be self sufficient, with bread baked, and butter and cream made in their own homes. Only sugar and salt had to be purchased. The farms had no gas, or electricity, and no central heating. The light was provided by kerosene lamps, the heating by coal or wood fires. No running water, father had to dig a well near the house for our drinking water, and another well near the meadow for the animals. No indoor toilet, we had to use a wooden cabin outside. During the night, we had chamber pots under each bed. To wash face and hands, we used a bowl filled with hot water from the kettle. The bath time, was in a zinc bath placed in front of the fire, and filled with water heated on the stove, in large bucket size container. Clothes were washed using a washboard in large oval wooden container filled with hot water. Without electricity, ironing of clothes had to be carried out by two solid metal irons heated on the stove, one at a time.

Village Hall and School

The Osadniks jointly built the above village hall and primary school, which I joined in September 1929. The new building had electricity, running water and telephone. Later on, it was extended, to accommodate a shop, Post Office, Savings Bank and Telephone Exchange. Later on, additional buildings were erected for storage of grain, milk dairy, and bakery.

My father, occasionally would ride to the market in Równe, to sell produce, animals and chickens. On his return home, he would tie the reins to the cart, tell his horses to go home and himself go to sleep. It was particularly useful in the winter, especially during snow blizzard, when father couldn't see anything. The horses always brought him home on sledges safely, managing carefully to turn from the road over the narrow wooden bridge, on to the drive leading to our house.

We had a continental climate, with hot summers and very cold winters, down to minus 20c, with lots of snow and snowstorms.

Many times our house was covered by snowdrifts right up to the roof with just the chimney being visible. After the snowstorm, we had to dig ourselves out from the front door up to the farmyard.

Father's second Marriage

After my mother died, the life for father became even more difficult, trying to run the farm and to look after three children, even though by now, he employed farm labourer, and a maid-cook/housekeeper.

Helena, Father, Stefan Bogusław (Boguś), Zofja, Danuta

In April 1931, he placed an advert in the National Newspaper for a wife. Father chose one applicant from Kraków, a 26-year-old postmistress, an unmarried mother with a four-year-old son, Ted (Tadeusz).

Without telling anyone, on 3rd of May, father travelled to Kraków and married Helena Ślusarczyk, on 5th May 1931. The next day, he returned home with Helena. Life on the farm was completely new to Helena, but she was soon helping with the running of the farm and joined the Osadniks Women's Association. Within a very short time, she became a very good farmer's wife and mother to the four children. Father adopted Ted as his son, and we called Helena, mother.

Helena was strict, but fair with us, without any preference for her son, Ted. Danuta got on very well with Helena, helped her with cooking and baking, and in her spare time, read books to her, as Helena's eyesight was weak. Helena's brother in Kraków, was only two years older than me, so I was receiving his outgrown town clothes, not very suitable to be worn on the farm, but, "Suitable for Sundays," Helena said.

I always hated those clothes, I thought they were sissy. As you can see in the above photo, I didn't look happy.

CHAPTER TWO

MY YOUNG DAYS AT OSADA

My father's name was Stefan, so I was called by abbreviated second name, Boguś. My father was appointed, Sołtys, (administrative head) of the Osada Krechowiecka.

After school, I made number of deliveries on my bike for my father to the Osadniks houses. Each farm had at least one or two guard dogs. A few times, I was bitten, and had my trousers torn by the dogs. Most of the time, I managed to defend myself with the large stick which I carried on the bike. I still have scars on my right hand from bites by one Alsatian dog, one scar 3 inches above the wrist, and second scar 3 inches above my elbow. In spite of the bites, I was not afraid of the dogs; most of them were not as ferocious as their barks. Eventually, I believed that I could handle even the bad dogs. At our farm, we had a guard dog, a type of Border collie, always chained to his kennel next to the stables door and the cow shed. During the night, the dog had a free run over the whole farmyard with his chain gliding on suspended wire. The dog recognized only my father as his master, even though he rarely fed him. Everybody was at risk; nobody could even stroke him without being bitten, except for Danuta, who claimed that the dog liked her. I was bitten once trying to stroke him after placing food in front of him. The 200 yards long drive-in to our farm from the main road, and over a small wooden bridge, was lined with the cherry trees. The dog would bark immediately any stranger crossed the bridge. The dog would go exceptionally wild whenever our usual Jewish merchant came to visit my father. We also had a little pet dog, white with black patches, called Luluś, who liked to follow me around, especially if I was on my bike. Whenever I had to go longer distances, I would order him to stay behind, but after a while, he would secretly follow me, hiding behind the trees and bushes.

My father once heard a young shepherd boy playing beautifully on his homemade violin, and decided that he would like me to learn to play violin.

He purchased a ¾-size second-hand instrument, and engaged a music teacher. I had no talent, but slowly I learned to play it.

Later on, my father bought me a full size second-hand violin.

My Uncle, Julian Mączka, built a house about 400 yards from our house at Karlowszczyzna, on land covered mostly by the trees designated for the common use of the Military Settlers. Uncle Julian lost a leg during the war, and was walking on a wooden prosthesis. He had two children, Edward, three years younger than me, and daughter, Henia. Uncle Julian liked fishing and hunting. He took me fishing a couple of times, but I found fishing rather boring, I could not keep still. I preferred to wander around the forest near the banks of the large river Horyń. Uncle Julian kept telling me to sit still, and not to scare his fish. In the end, he refused to take me fishing, but I was rather pleased about that. One night, Uncle Julian took me hunting, and he warned me to stay quiet and to keep still. Suddenly, I spotted a big stag in front of me; I involuntarily jumped and the stag run away, my Uncle was annoyed that I scared his stag: "I told you to keep still or I won't take you hunting again." Uncle explained that the stag got near us because we were standing against the wind blowing from the stag. I was disappointed a little about his decision.

One day, my father asked me to collect a parcel from the Post Office. On arrival, I was told that the parcel had not arrived. Whilst returning home on my bike, it started raining. The road paved by granite cobblestones, became very slippery. Suddenly, I heard a bus behind me. The next thing I remember was walking into our farm courtyard, pushing the bike, with the front wheel twisted, and a bent handlebar. Waiting at the gate, were father and Danuta. My father asked, "Where is the parcel?" I replied, "What parcel?" I lost my memory. Next morning I did recollect cycling to the Post Office, remembered cycling back and hearing the bus coming behind me. I must have had a concussion, because to this day I don't remember how the accident happened, and how I walked the one mile back home.`

I was a member of the local Scouts Group; I remember camping in the forest on the bank of the river Horyń. Whilst swimming, I got myself in difficulties and I was drowning, but was saved by the Scout leader, Mr. Korusiewicz.

Boarding School

In 1936, I obtained a scholarship to the Grammar School, Gimnazjum Tadeusza Kościuszki No. 709, in Równe 10 miles (15kl) from my home. During the first school year, 1936/37, I was boarded in the Army Barracks, pending construction of Bursa, the residence for students, with few other students. I only remember Ted Nowicki and Krystyna Gałkowska from those days. Distance from Army Barracks to above school was about 1 mile. Równe, the capital of the District of Wołyń in 1931, had 41,900 inhabitants, of which 65% were Jews. Although only 12% of the Jews lived in the whole of the County, in most of the towns they represented 60-70% of the population. To my knowledge and local experience, we had good relations with the Jews in Równe, and in other neighbouring towns.

Stefan Bogusław in 1938, wearing school blazer with Scout badge

Równe 1939

View of the Parish Church Ul. 3 Maja, (now Soborna)

From left. Danuta, Zofia, Helena in 1939

In the meantime, the Osadniks Association started building a Bursa (Hall of Residence) for students. The first wing on the left of the photograph below, had accommodation for boys. The adjoining taller building the Osadnik Gimnazjum, with plans for 2nd wing on the right, for girls accommodation. The Bursa was nearer to my Grammar school, which was only about 300 yards away. The hall of residence was a modern building, with all facilities right up to-date. Each bedroom had 4 beds and bedside cabinets only. At the end of the corridor were toilets, communal shower room and wall lined with lockable cupboards, one for each student.

On the left, Bursa accommodation for boys, in 1937

Taller building on the right, the Osadniks Gimnazjum, in 1938

At my Grammar School, I joined the symphony orchestra as a lead violinist; I also joined the Bursa Brass Band.

Bursa's Festival of Song, Music and Sport at Grodno, May 1939. I am third from the left, holding a clarinet

During vacations, I was teaching a girl to play the violin, she was one year younger than me; the money was useful to supplement my pocket money. The pretty young lady was more interested in me than in her violin, so I put an end to the lessons. At that time, I was not interested in any girls. I was a very keen sportsman; I liked throwing discus, javelin and shot put, long jump, running, boxing, playing basketball, netball, rugby and boxing. In sports competition, I run in 4x400 meters relay. During the winter, I preferred ice skating and skiing. During my school years I did not smoke and I was not interested in girls, although there were girls in my Grammar School. I took part in walking holidays during the summer, organized by the Bursa. In 1938, I walked for one month in the Vilno region. In 1939, I walked in the Eastern Carpathian Mountains. The main purpose of those holidays was to get to know Eastern Poland.

My father's farm

By 1937, life was getting better for my father. He employed permanently two loyal, long serving servants, John and Maria. In addition, he used a casual labour from nearby village of Koźlin.

I remember more than once driving a horse cart to the village of Koźlin. The cart length was extended with a long ladder on each side and filled in the middle with the straw. I usually collected about 6-10 women to help with various jobs as required. The young Ukrainian women dressed in the embroidered blouses and skirts, were singing during the journey and whilst working. Sometimes, if required, they stayed the night sleeping in the hayloft above the stables.

I remember looking at the long line of women singing whilst weeding the two acres field of sugar beet. Mother Helena, in the first row making sure that they managed to keep up with her. The sugar beet was grown for the near-by Sugar Factory.

Father had 6 cows and a stud bull, 3 horses, a few pigs, a flock of sheep, number of chickens, turkeys, ducks, geese and rabbits. Our ram, with big curving horns, was in the habit of butting everybody in sight who was bending down. A number of times, I had been his unwilling victim, until one day when Danuta called out: "The ram's behind you." I lifted the back of jacket over my head, and bending down, I turned round to face the ram. To my surprise, the ram stopped immediately, just a few feet from me. Next time the ram charged me, providing I had heard him, and had time to repeat my trick , it worked every time.

Father purchased a horse drawn harvester for cutting down the crops of wheat, oats and barley, and a horse drawn grass cutter for cutting hay in the meadow. Previously, the crops and hay had to be cut by hand with a scythe.

In addition to general farming, father diversified in to tobacco plantation Virginia for cigarettes and Kentucky for cigars. Father constructed a wooden shed, heated for drying of tobacco leaves. Tobacco leaves threaded on the long string were hung in the rafters of the barn to partly dry, before transfer to heated shed.

Tobacco provided extra employment in autumn for farm labour.

Dried tobacco leaves had to be sorted and baled for delivery to the State Monopoly Tobacco factory. Not even a single leaf of tobacco could be retained for private use. Penalty: loss of grower's license.

Father started an orchard by planting six acres of fruit trees.

Father purchased four beehives to help pollinate the fruit trees, and to provide us with honey. I helped father with the bees, and we were bitten many times resulting in swollen hands and faces. After a time we both got so used to being bitten, that the bites didn't produce any swelling.

Father employed workers to dig up a fishpond in the meadow for the carp, near the well for the cattle, and the large pine tree. The pond was not deep, so I could catch a carp for dinner easily with the net.

The next big project was building a kiln at the end of our meadow for production of bricks. Father employed the experienced brick-maker, who built the kiln for firing bricks; father also provided a horse for churning up clay. Father made a deal with the Forestry Commission; in exchange for wood to fire the kiln, he promised to supply them bricks. The new health centre near the church was also built with father's bricks. Soon after, Father started building a new house using his own bricks, with labour carried out by Students from Krzemieniec School of Building, who at that time were constructing a Parish church for the settlers 300 yards from our house.

Our house was completed in 1938

Grandmother Salomea

The Mączka house is the only Osadniks house remaining. This neglected house is owned by one woman. All other Military Settlers homes in eastern Poland had been demolished. Our Village Hall, School and all associated buildings, were also demolished. Stalin succeeded in his revenge to obliterate every trace of the Osadnik Military Settlers.

Kościół w Karłowszczyźnie na Wołyniu, zbudowany przez osadników wojskowych z osad: Krechowieckiej, Hallerowo, Jazłowieckiej i Bajonówki

The church built by settlers from four neighbouring Osadas, completed in 1938

It was a big project; the foundations were dug by the settlers. The stones, sand and lime collected from the quarry by horse carts, with great help from the local villagers. The first parish priest was father Jan Kąkol, ordained in 1937. Osadniks purchased Uncle Julian's house for a presbytery for father Kąkol. The church was only a short stroll from our house. Couple of times, I was asked by a priest to play violin during the mass at the new church. I remember previous Sunday's masses at a chapel in Horyngród, the settlers, driving horse carriages in the summer, and the sledges in the winter, with bells jingling round the horse's necks. Now my family had to walk only 300 hundred yards to the new church. Christmas Eve was a great family occasion; preparing an evening meal consisting of 12 dishes, no meat, mainly fish.

The Christmas tree decorated with the candles, lit at the first sight of the star in the sky, we would sit at the table soon after. This was a once a year occasion when our servants would join us at the table. In accordance with the tradition, there was always a one empty place set aside for an unexpected traveller/visitor. After the meal, we would open the presents from under the Christmas tree, and sing carols. The table covered with white tablecloth, a little hay and straw were placed under it. My father would draw a straw and tell the fortune for each of us. At about 11 pm, we would drive to Horyngród chapel for a midnight mass. At the new church,

Father Kąkol conducted the last mass on Christmas Eve in 1939, attended by some of the remaining settlers. In 1943, the Red Army again entered Polish borders, fighting the retreating Germans; bombarded the church with the local population sheltering inside. The ruined church stonework and bricks, were later plundered by the locals.

The Soviets built a pigsty on the remaining foundations of the church.

Photo of the Pigsty by SB. Maczka, September 1995

During the summer and other school holidays, I helped my father on the farm. Also, I helped in the brickworks, checking the loading of the bricks on horse drawn carts, and issuing sales invoices. I loved walking to the nearby forest to collect mushrooms and blueberries, and to bathe in the river Horyń flowing through the forest. I also liked cycling.

The small stream trickling slowly through our meadows, would flood in the autumn the whole of the meadows, producing a frozen lake on which I enjoyed ice-skating. During the last three years, I preferred skiing. One day, I found a baby deer apparently lost from its mother. I carried him home, and Danuta fed him from a milk bottle. The deer was growing fast and was very friendly; he had a run of the whole farm, but would always come when called. Unfortunately, by running and jumping was damaging the tobacco plants. As he was now fully grown, I took him to the forest, trying to leave him behind, but he kept on following me back home. On the third attempt, I managed to leave the lovable deer in the forest. On my return, I found my two sisters crying and worrying about their pet.

In 1932, Poland signed the 10-year non-aggression pact with the Soviet Union, and in 1934, a similar pact with Germany. In August 1939, two 18-year-old aunties arrived for one-month vacation. The twins, Czesia and Halina Mączka, one year older than me, from Skarzysko-Kamienna, which is near to Starachowice.

They managed to return home, just before the war started on 1st September 1939.

CHAPTER THREE

WAR AND DEPORTATION TO SIBERIA

POPULATIONS AND SIZES

GERMANY
78,5 →
Million People

POLAND
35,1
Million People

USSR
← 175,5
Million People

Shown below the enormous size of the Soviet Union

Small Poland was sandwiched between Germany in the west, and the USSR in the east.

Population of Germany 78.5 million.

Poland 35.1 million.

USSR 175.5 million.

23 August 1939, an Official pact of non-aggression was signed in Moscow, by Ribbentrop- Molotow, which included a secret agreement to partition

Poland on 26th August, along the Curzon Line, although the Curzon Line proposal in 1920, had been rejected by Soviets. Poland signed Alliance Pact with France on 24th August, and with England, on 25th August 1939.

23rd August 1939 Molotov signing the Agreement with Ribbentrop

1st September 1939, 1.5 million Germans invaded Poland without declaring war. Poles defended bravely with 700,000 soldiers.

Germans were much better armed, with more airplanes and tanks.

The Soviets, I believe possibly remembering defeat in 1920, waited before attacking Poland, to see how the Germans got on.

3rd September, I heard on the radio that Britain declared war on Germany. This was a great news, but my father said, that if Poland's warning in 1933 to France and England about rearmament by Germans, (in contradiction of the Versailles agreement) was acted on, the German attack on Poland would have been prevented. Winston Churchill was trying to persuade the British government about the danger of German rearmament, but he was ignored and labelled a warmonger. Now the expected immediate attack by France and Britain on Germans to help Poland, did not happen.

The Polish army fiercely fought the invading, much better armed Germans, for 35 days, inflicting heavy losses. Germans lost 50,000 dead, Polish losses were greater, 66,300 killed, 133,700 wounded, and 420,000 taken as prisoners of war.

On 17th September, without declaring war, the Red Army crossed the Polish borders. The Soviet attack was totally unexpected, a treacherous stab in the back. In spite of the attack from the east by the Soviets, the Polish forces continued to fight Germans. On 27th September, Warsaw capitulated. But Poland had not surrendered to the Germans. Poland had not ceased to exist, and vowed to continue the fight for independence. Polish Government retreated to Rumunia, where they were interned, as unexpectedly Rumunia decided to support Germany.

Some of the remaining army units and individual soldiers, escaped to friendly Hungary, then, on to France and England. Number of Polish navy ships managed to escape to Scotland. Many pilots managed to fly to England. Other pilots via Hungary, also managed to reach England. The new Polish Government in exile was set-up in London to continue the fight against Germany. In the morning of 17 September, I heard on the radio in our house, a broadcast in Polish from the Soviet Union, announcing that their forces had crossed Polish borders.

"We are coming to help Poland fight Germans. Do not offer resistance. We are coming as your friends."

Noticing the Red Army marching, I walked to the roadside. Our Osada was about 20 miles from the border with the Soviet Union. The column stopped for a rest. I was astonished to see so many soldiers poorly equipped and dressed. A number of them carried old rifles hanging over their shoulders tied with string, and had no proper boots or uniforms. Our new house was about 200 yards from the road, its new zinc roof shining in the sun, the drive-in lined with cherry trees. The officer leading the column asked, "Whose is this house? It must be kułak." (Rich peasant or farmer). I replied, "It is my father's house, but he is not a Kułak." Without further comment, the soldiers resumed their march. I found leaflets dropped by the Soviet planes: "During the last few days, the Polish army has been destroyed. Over 60,000 Soldiers have voluntarily come over to our side from the following towns: Tarnopol. Galicz, Równe, Dubno, Soldiers! What is left for you? Why are you risking your life? Your resistance is futile. Officers are pushing you to a senseless slaughter. They hate you and your families. It is they who have shot your delegates, which you have sent to us with the proposal of surrender. Don't believe your officers. Officers and generals are your enemies, they want you dead. Believe us! Red Army is your only friend."

Signed: S. Timoshenko, the Commander of the Red Army Ukrainian front. Next day, NKVD officials, later called KGB, arrived in our area requesting surrender of all arms, and then started to set up a Soviet administration. Firstly, NKVD appointed Soviet party activists to higher administrative positions. 22nd October, NKVD organized the Local Elections, disfranchising most of the Polish population; Communist candidates were selected by NKVD, most of them not known to the local population. With my father's encouragement, our two servants attended the local meetings. Tens of thousands of Polish soldiers and officers, managed to escape through Hungary and Rumania to France, and some to England, to continue fighting Germans for freedom of Poland.

Partition of Poland. In 1939 Germans took the west side of Poland

USSR took the East Poland along the Curzon Line.

Germans and Soviets made territorial adjustment in order to adhere strictly to the borders along the Curzon Line. The German part of Polish land contained 22 million people, which were now declared to be German citizens. The Soviets occupied Polish land contained 13 million people, which were now declared to be Soviet citizens. Soviets took 190,000 Polish soldiers as prisoners.

Burying the Standard and Valuables

In the evening, Mr. Boleslaw Podhorski came to see my father carrying a long parcel wrapped in material covered with tar. Father called me to fetch a spade and go with Mr. Podhorski to bury the parcel at the cemetery located near the church, and about 300 yards from our house. It was getting dark, we went to the grave of the pilot Kąkol, who was killed in a plane crash. The pilot was the brother of our parish priest.

A propeller was attached to the very large, tall upright granite headstone. The grave itself, was covered by a large granite slab. I dug a hole under the slab at the foot of the grave, about eighteen inches deep, by three feet long. I buried the parcel containing a duplicate Standard of the 1st Krechowiecki Lancers Regiment. It was donated by the regiment to our Osada, and was hanging by the altar of our new church. On return home, my father decided to bury his rifle, hunting gun, revolver and ammunition, including the silver cutlery, which was Helena's dowry. Father oiled the weapons, and wrapped them up separately in tar-covered materials. The silver cutlery was also wrapped separately. We buried the parcels under the large pine tree located about 300 ft from the house next to six beehives.

Eviction from our farm

Our two long serving and loyal servants had reported confidentially to father that the land would be taken from all Military Settlers without any compensation. Officials will arrive shortly to take stock of the farms. The settlers will be allowed to take with them only personal possessions.

My father put the following suggestion to his two servants: "When the NKVD officials arrive to take the inventory, tell them that I was a very bad employer, you had not been paid for a number of years, but I had promised to give you my cows and horses. Would you also ask them if between you, you could be allowed to run the farm until the collectivization of the land. I am sure that you will be believed. I am asking a favour that after my eviction, you would bring to me some supplies from the farm?" They replied, "Yes."

On arrival at Bursa, I found that my place had been taken by the son of a local communist official.

My father then took me to his friends, Mr. & Mrs. Bodzak. He was a railway man, his wife Zofja, was a sister of Mrs. Wanda Cała, our very good friend and neighbour. After securing the lodgings, I was able to continue at my Grammar School. In the meantime, my family; father Stefan, mother Helena, sisters Danuta and Zofja, brother Ted and grandmother Salomea, (mother of my father), were evicted from the farm with just a few personal possessions. Father found accommodation in friendly Jew's house in Tuczyn, 5 km (3 miles) away from our farm. The servants, as promised, delivered food at night: 2 sacks of flower, a barrel of salted pork, beef, container of lard, smoked legs of ham, smoked sausages, milk, churn full of honey, etc.

My family, and all the Osadniks, were ordered to report weekly to the local police, so they could keep a close check on us.

Father's escape to his birthplace

In January 1940, my father with his friend and neighbour, Vincent Cała, decided to explore the conditions in the part of Poland occupied by Germany. They were heading for Starachowice; the hometown of father's family 120 miles south of Warsaw. The German border guards caught them, and handed them to the Russians. On their second attempt, they were successful. Father wrote to say that for us, it would be better to live under Germans than Russians, and that he would come for us soon. On the 8th of February 1940, father arrived at my accommodation, tired after the long journey. Next morning, we travelled to our family in Tuczyn, about 13 miles from Równe, it was a great joy to be reunited.

Deportation to Siberia

Next day, the 10th of February 1940, at 6 am, we were woken-up by banging on our door. The NKVD official in civilian clothes, accompanied by two Ukrainian militiamen armed with rifles, read out a Deportation Order, giving us two hours to pack, telling us, "Take warm clothes and tools, such as axes, saws etc." My father asked, "Are we being deported to Siberia?" He replied, "Yes." Then he departed, leaving two militiamen to supervise us. After two hours, the NKVD officer returned. The sledges were waiting for us. My grandmother fainted, acting on previous instruction from Father. Father explained to the NKVD man, that his mother was not capable to travel, as she had a very weak heart. To our surprise, he allowed her to stay behind. Grandmother planned to return to the farm now run by the servants, and to continue as a housekeeper to the parish priest Jan Kąkol, for whom she worked before eviction from the farm. Our family was loaded on the first sledge, the luggage on the second sledge. We were lucky that we were allowed to take quite a lot of food with us. It was a very cold winter, minus 20-30c, with snow two feet deep. Our little pet dog, Luluś, followed us for a while, but could not cope with the deep snow. We were herded in the cattle wagons; our larger luggage was put in the last wagon. We spent two days at Lubomirka Station, whilst NKVD collected more people in the area. Next day, 12 February at approximately 6.30am. we arrived at Równe station. More deportees were loaded onto our train. Later on, two people per wagon were allowed out to collect water and coal. I took a bucket for water to be collected from the pump in front of the station. We were followed by a Russian soldier. As I started pumping water, the passenger train arrived with a lot of students from my Grammar School, all walking by the pump. On the spur of the moment, I took off my overcoat, holding it under my arm and exposing my school uniform, I mingled with the crowd of my schoolmates. I then walked to my nearby lodgings. I informed Mrs. Zofja Bodzak, to her great surprise, that my family was being deported to Siberia, together with other Osadniks. I only came to collect my belongings for the journey; Zofja said "What about your skis and violin?" I replied, "There is no room in the wagon." This was my opportunity to stay behind, but without any hesitation, I returned with a packed suitcase to the station. The soldier on guard would not allow me near the train, but after explaining that I had left the train only to collect my clothes, the soldier called the NKVD officer who unlocked the sliding door of the wagon and called my father to identify me, before letting me to join my family. On the 10th of February 1940, the first transport of 140,000-150,000 deportees to Siberia, were middle classes, and almost all Osadniks including their families, approx. 45,000. This was Stalin's revenge for his defeat in 1920. Stalin decided to destroy Polish Nation both physically and culturally. Also deported were the Forest Rangers, but the majority of deportees were the middle class intelligentsia, solicitors, judges, doctors, teachers, university professors, and policemen all being classified by Soviets, as enemies of the people, namely, kulaks, landowners, and capitalists. Further deportations took place on 13 April 1940, and 29 June 1940.

Please note, that after invasion by Germany, about 300,000 middle class Jews escaped from western to eastern Poland. Most were also deported.

In the last transport on 29 June 1941, were mostly middle class Jews. For the first time, the men were separated from women.

The total of 1,200,000 civilians was deported from Eastern Poland. The 190,000 Polish soldiers as prisoners of war, were not included in this number, neither the refugees from western Poland. Next day at the Soviet Union border, we were transferred to wider gauge Soviet cattle train, the wagons were bigger and wider than Polish ones.

FLOOR PLAN OF CATTLE WAGON

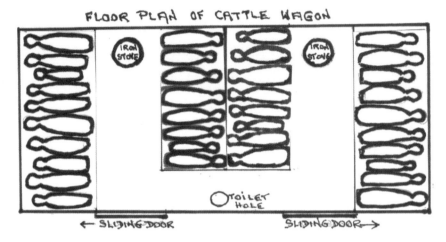

NKVD crammed 72 people into each of those cattle wagons

Each wagon had two sliding doors on each side. At each end, there were two levels of wooden planks, allowing 10 people to sleep like sardines on one level. 20 people at each end of the wagon. In the middle of the wagon, between two doors, was a hole in the floor for the toilet. Parents hung a blanket to provide a privacy screen. So, there was less room in the middle for wooden bunks, which could accommodate only 32 people. The personal luggage was placed below the bottom layer. Each wagon had two iron stoves, burning wood or coal for heating and cooking. The total number in our cattle wagon was 72, including my friends from school with their parents. We took over the top right hand bunk: Tadek Nowicki, Krysia Gałkowska, Stasia Kolacz, myself, Danuta. I don't remember the names of the other three?

The NKVD personnel, and the armed guards were travelling more comfortably, in the passenger wagon.

Drawn by deportee M. Kuczyński

Drawn by my friend, deportee M. Kuczyński

In defiance of the NKVD, and the Soviet soldiers guarding us, we were singing patriotic songs. During rare stops at the stations, nobody was allowed out, except two persons per wagon to bring water and coal. At some stations, we were lucky to receive bread and bucket of soup to be shared with everybody in the wagon. The temperature outside was minus 35-40c. The wagons were heated by coal burning small stoves; we had to wrap ourselves well to keep warm. Danuta who slept on the top bunk next to the wall remembers:

"My hair froze to the wall." The travelling conditions in those locked cattle trains crammed with people without room to move, no privacy, no washing and no toilet facilities, were absolutely awful. 138 Polish deportees had described their own personal experiences fully in the book translated into English. Danuta describes her own story on pages 202 to 206. The Book, was published in year 2000, by The Association of Osadniks Children, of which I am a proud member for the last 26 years. Due to the great demand, this book was reprinted in 2007 and in 2009. The book is advertised on the Internet. Comparing my experiences with deportees from other parts of Eastern Poland, I found that a lot of them were treated very much worse than my family. It depended largely on the attitude of NKVD, and local communist officials. Some deportees were robbed of all personal possessions and valuables and not allowed to take anything with them.

Arrival in Siberia

After travelling for 17 days, we arrived on 27 February, at Kotlas, in Arkhangelsk region. The entire train was unloaded at the school opposite the station. Our larger luggage was also unloaded. We had to sleep on the floor amongst our belongings; it was crowded, and children were crying.

In the morning, the sledges drawn by horses arrived. The NKVD, called out family names to be loaded on the sledges. My family, not being called, had to spend another night in the school. Next morning, mother Helena was taken ill with a high temperature, the doctor diagnosed pneumonia. She was admitted to the local hospital. My family was taken on two sledges during a snowstorm and temperature of -40C to Privodino 14 miles away. We spent the night in the Orthodox Church, (Converted into a Club).

The journey from Kotlas was over flat open ground covered by snow. Due to the snowstorm, I did not see any trees, houses or villages.

CHAPTER FOUR

LIFE AND WORK IN SIBERIA

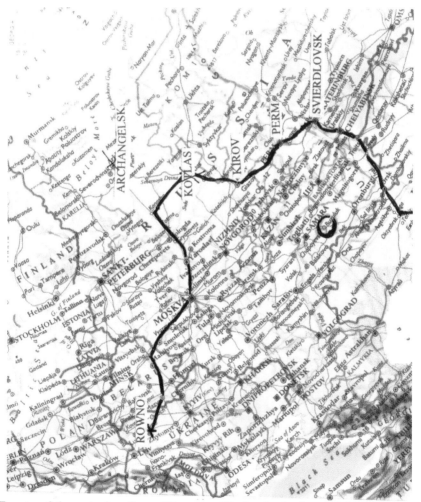

Route of deportation from Równe to Kotlas in Archangelsk area

Map of specposioleks near Kotlas

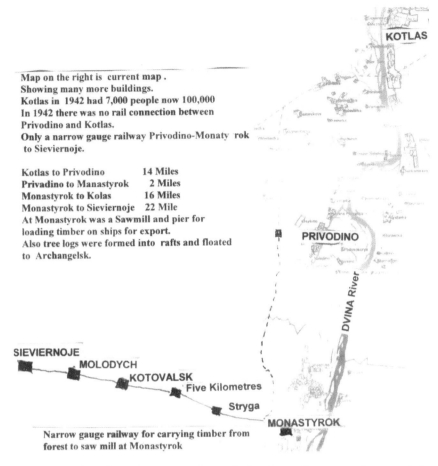

Map on the right is current map .
Showing many more buildings.
Kotlas in 1942 had 7,000 people now 100,000
In 1942 there was no rail connection between
Privodino and Kotlas.
Only a narrow gauge railway Privodino-Monaty rok
to Sieviernoje.

Kotlas to Privodino   14 Miles
Privadino to Manastyrok   2 Miles
Monastyrok to Kolas   16 Miles
Monastyrok to Sieviernoje   22 Mile
At Monastyrok was a Sawmill and pier for
loading timber on ships for export.
Also tree logs were formed into rafts and floated
to Archangelsk.

KOTLAS

PRIVODINO

DVINA River

SIEVIERNOJE

MOLODYCH

KOTOVALSK

Five Kilometres

Stryga

MONASTYROK

Narrow gauge railway for carrying timber from
forest to saw mill at Monastyrok

The railway line from Stryga, ran through the dense forest, made up mainly from pine and spruce trees.

The following morning, on 21st February, we boarded a narrow gauge railway at Privodino and travelled deep into the forest. Arriving in the evening at a posiołek (work camp), called Kotovalsk. Comprising of four

wooden barracks, a small shop and a communal kitchen, all buildings were constructed from logs. Together with other families, we were crammed into one of the larger barracks. Camp Commandant, called a meeting and informed us that we will never return to Poland, and everybody age 15 and over, must work hard to earn his or her living.

In the morning of 6th March, all men were ordered to work in the forest.

They were issued with axes and saws and promised to be paid for work done, but there was nothing to buy in the shop. Father was given a pass to visit Helena in Kotlas hospital, and a number of friends gave him money for shopping.

My sister, Danuta, remembers cooking for eight, from the provisions brought with us from Poland, mainly noodles, to be shared with Mr. & Mrs. Gałkowski, their daughter, Krystyna, and son, Grzesio. After a week, our parents returned. Helena was very weak and tired after the journey. Father was very upset to report that all the money was stolen from him in the queue to the canteen. The people who gave him the money were very angry. Father promised them, "I will work hard to repay you." Note: In England, in March 2008, I spoke with Kristina Gałkowska about this stolen money. To Danuta's and my great surprise, she informed me that her father called a meeting of all those who suffered the loss, and that he fully repaid each one of them from his own pocket.

All Osadniks, as farmers, were used to hard work. The work in the forest, lumbering, felling trees in the snow two feet deep, and with the temperature -30c or -40c, was very hard. We had to work extra hard in order to use a lot of energy to keep warm, otherwise, we would just freeze to death.

My sister Danuta remembers the date, 21st March, which was her 15th birthday. She also remembers Easter. Using her own words: "On Saturday before Easter, we cleaned the barrack and decorated with fir tree branches so that it would be nice and festive. We managed to buy an egg, but we were missing a priest. On Easter day, with a drop of holy water I brought from home, my father blessed that egg, cut it into minute pieces, said a prayer, and shared it between us, and some of our near companions in adversity. We all prayed very sincerely to God and the Holy Mother of Częstochowa, asking for a change to our fate. Everybody is crying. Our first Easter in exile is very sad."

In the afternoon, we were moved by sledges, 3 miles to Station Mołodych. This posiolek was a little better than previous ones; there were wooden walkways between barracks, a shop with nothing to sell, and a canteen. There was also a Doctor's surgery with a pretty young nurse.

Our barrack in Molodych, accommodated 3 families. Gałkowski, four people. Oleś, six, and Mączka six. Danuta's note: "We now have a family bunk bed; we no longer have to sleep on the floor."

Danuta also remembers; that next day on Easter Monday, a Camp Commandant ordered her to go to work with the others, "You are now 15 years of age." The girls refused as it was Easter. Next day, the girls were ordered to clear snow from the railway line. After working all day, Danuta's back and hands were aching. She was paid 3 roubles.

My father and I continued to work in the forest, cutting down the trees. The pay was extremely low, well below the subsistence level, but so far, we were managing on the provisions from Poland.

Nadia, a pretty 18-year-old girl from Moscow, and a friend of the doctor's nurse, was seconded along with her to work in administration in Siberia for two years. Nadia took a liking to me. I don't know why. I hadn't given her any encouragement. She would turn up most evenings in our barrack with a guitar, and sing love songs to me in the presence of my family. I was very embarrassed about it.

I considered that, as a Pole, I should not associate with the Russian girl. My friends were pulling my leg about her; I suspect that they were possibly a little jealous, as she was pretty, and a good singer.

From 10th April, Danuta had no more snow to clear, it was not snowing, so she was given work in the forest, gathering branches from the felled trees and stacking them up in piles, which were then set on fire. The forest regulations required workers to burn all the branches on the ground during the winter, in order to reduce the danger of forest fires during the dry summer.

Work in the Sawmill at Monastyrok

On 15th April, snow began to melt. With a number of other families, we were moved out from the forest by a train drawn by a Polish locomotive. We arrived out of the forest, at a bigger posiołek named Monastyrok, situated by the large river Dvina, about two miles from Privodino.

Danuta describes her first impressions: "The camp was surrounded by tall wooden stockade with guard tower on each corner, and an enormous entrance gate, which looks to me like a prison. It frightens me. I soon discovered that there are no guards in the towers, and the gate is shut and locked only at night."

The name Monastyrok, is derived from the Orthodox Church still standing with the cross on its tower. The ex-church was now used as a storeroom, shop, canteen and the school for children.

Each family had been allocated separate quarters. Our family of six, was given a large room with two bunk beds, separate small kitchen with a tiny cellar below. The room was located near the entrance gate. Danuta commented: "Comparing with previous accommodation it is quite comfortable." One hundred families of deportees were housed in this camp. Talking to others, I discovered that our accommodation was better than average.

There was a problem with bed bugs. The wooden beds and wooden walls were infested with them, coming out in the night to bite us. There was no way of getting rid of those horrible bugs.

In charge of the camp, was NKVD commandant, Kpt. Organ, with a deputy, Lt. Rogaczewski. Kpt. Organ told us: "This is now your home; you will never return to Poland, you must adapt yourselves to the permanent life here. You must work to earn your living. If you don't work, you don't eat. (Nie rabotaj nie kushaj). You can't leave the work camp without pass from me. The population here in towns and villages, is made up mostly from Russians exiled here during the Tsarists rule, and by the present Soviet Government." Kpt. Organ stated, "They are now happily settled Siberians.

My father on the other hand, was encouraging everybody to believe that, "Eventually we will get away from this hell, and return to Poland. We had lost everything, but we must look after our health."

Father also organized weekly dances to encourage young ones to keep their spirits up. Most of the adults called him an optimist, but I believe that most of the young ones shared his optimism.

According to the official Soviet terminology, Monastyrok was not a labour camp, but a specposiołek, or 'special' settlement. The difference, was that corrective labour camps, called Gulags, were reserved for people sentenced by court to loss of liberty. Whilst deportees were sent without a court hearing, to 'special' settlements, which were reserved for those for whom a different kind of restricted liberty was arranged. Special settlement, equated to free labour, as opposed to penal labour in Gulags without pay.

I consider from personal experience, that pay at specposiołek was so low, that most of the Russian people would starve if they couldn't achieve the targets or Stachanov norms.

In Gulags, there was no pay for work, the food rations were based on achieving Stachanov norms. Those who managed to achieve norms would just survive on their rations; non-achievers would slowly die on reduced amount of food. The mortality rates in Gulags were very high, but dead were quickly replaced by the new inmates.

The human life in Soviet Union was cheap and expendable commodity. One evening, we were summoned to the meeting. The Communist political Commissar proclaimed proudly, that, "The Soviet Union is a worker's paradise, there is no unemployment, everybody has a job." He then quoted a slogan; "If you don't work, you don't eat." He also said, "That the poor workers in the Capitalist countries are exploited." Apparently, the Stachanov norms were started in Coal mining, now operating in every type of manual work. The Stachanov norms in lumber jacking, had been set up by a big, strong Russian, cutting down large trees without any undergrowth to clear in record time, and producing record number of cubic meters of timber. This norm was expected to be achieved by all lumberjacks. In practice, this was impossible; as we had to first clear all undergrowth, including young trees, which were not taken into account during measurement of work done. To illustrate his point about the exploitation of workers in America, the Commissar showed us a film of workers digging trenches. A big strong American in front setting up a standard of work, the workers that could not keep up with him, were paid less.

I, and everybody else in the room could see no difference between digging trenches in America and Stachanov norms, which blatantly exploited the Soviet workers. We believed that even the slowest American trench diggers were probably paid better then the Soviet achievers of Stachanov norms, but it was not safe for us to express our opinions. The local Russian population comprising mostly deportees sent to Siberia during the Tsarist and Soviet rule were informed by NKVD that we were deported here because we were kulaks, (rich peasants). They should not believe our stories that life was better in Poland, because we, as kulaks, by exploiting the poor peasants, certainly had a better life. Outside the camp by the river, was a large sawmill, in which most of our people, including my sister Danuta had to work. Some of the deportees were assigned to work at collective farms. Two girls were working at Privodino Hospital.

My father and I were part of the gang building log houses.

4ft tree stumps were placed in the holes dug in the soil down to solid frozen ground into the perma frost, about 2 feet deep.

The tree stumps 2ft above ground, formed a base for the foundation of the house. We had to cut the logs for the floor and walls; we had to saw logs for wooden planks to make doors and windows, using only wooden nails. The joints between logs, floorboards, windows and doors were packed with moss to insulate from drafts.

Other than to work, we were not allowed to leave our quarters without a pass from the NKVD. Bread rations were given only to workers and to children too young to work.

The timber cut in the forest during the winter, was moved in the spring to the sawmill by rail. I was separated from my father and assigned to the gang of men whose job was to unload manually the tree logs (2-5meters long) from the wagons. We worked in 12-hour shifts, for five days with one day's rest, meaning that very seldom our rest day happened on Sunday. It was a very hard work.

Communist propaganda broadcasted that: "Soviet Union was a Worker's Paradise; the Soviet workers had to work only five days a week, whereas workers in the west had a six day working week."

In reality I believed that the sole purpose of working five days and resting on sixth day was to make sure that most Sundays were a working days. In order to disrupt the religion already oppressed heavily by closure of most of the churches in the Soviet Union.

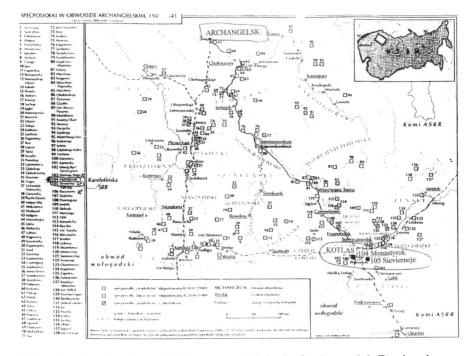

Map showing location of 138 specposiołeks in Archangelsk Region in the north-west USSR, in 1940

In the top right corner of this plan, is map of the Soviet Union. Look out for the little white rectangle representing just an Archangelsk Region. Gulags were not shown on the above map. The specposiołeks and Gulags were scattered all over Siberia, and some specposioleks were also in Kazakhstan region. It is believed that about 18-21 million people were held in forced labour camps, Gulags, and in specposiołeks. Due to very high mortality rate, particularly in Gulags, it was impossible to verify any of the figures, even with KGB records at Kremlin now available. Human life in the Soviet Union at that time was very cheap and expendable. It is alleged that 20 million died in the Gulags and specposioleks during the Stalin's rule. Highest death rate was by starvation, ill-treatment and cold in Gulags, but dead workers were quickly replaced by new inmates. Danuta recollects in her diary, "In June 1940, mother made a little garden under our window, planted vegetables, potatoes, onions, cucumbers and beans. Everything was growing very fast during hot summer days almost 22 hours long."

School Propaganda

My sister Zofia and my brother Ted with other Polish children were attending a local school. After returning home, they reported that the teacher asked children if they believed in God. Only Polish children raised their hands. The teacher then asked them to pray for bread. After a short wait. Teacher said, "No bread no God."

"Who believes in Stalin?" Russian children raised their hands. Teacher asked them to pray to Stalin for bread. Immediately a woman entered the classroom carrying a tray with slices of bread, given only to children who prayed to Stalin.

I do not know if this was practiced in other schools in the Soviet Union. Bread and food were rationed; Rye bread (without butter) was more valuable to a Russian than a cake to the child in the west. During my time in the Soviet Union, I never saw white bread, cakes or butter.

According to the schoolbooks, all the discoveries in science and medicines were made by the Russians. Citizens of the Soviet Union were completely isolated from any information from the West. No radio transmission from the West no books were allowed. Ordinary citizens were not allowed to travel or work outside their region without permit from NKVD. Not allowed to travel west. This way the Soviet propaganda was believed by most of their people.

Nadia was writing letters to me, to which I was not replying.

Separated from my family to work in Sieviernoje

The first snow fell in September 1940. The nights were now getting very much longer, but illuminated by moon, stars and polar lights so the nights were not dark.

In October I was selected with Stanisław Zaręba, Janina Oleś and Stasia Kołacz to work with local Russians in the posiołek called Sieviernoje about 35 km (22 miles) from Monastyrok. Situated at the end of the narrow gauge railway line, deep in the fir and pine forest. We shared the log barrack with eight Russian men; each of us had a wooden bed, with a straw filled mattress and pillow.

In the middle of a barrack was a wooden barrel containing drinking water, and at each end of the barrack was a wood burning fire. The barrack was infested with horrible bed bugs.

Shortly after our arrival, a large group of single young Russian men and women were seconded to work in this settlement. They were placed in two adjoining barracks, men separated from women.

Each of us was ordered to work with one of the Russian gangs of four men to cut trees. In the morning, we had to walk briskly in order to keep warm for about half a mile over open deforested land to our place of work in the forest. Snow was knee deep, it was very cold, on average minus 35c but it felt much colder if the wind was blowing. After a while we would point out to each other, "Your nose is white." And we would pick up snow in gloved hand, and rub the nose, and quite quickly the circulation was restored. We were dressed in quilted jacket with sweater, shirt and vest under it, quilted trousers with long johns. Fur lined hats over our heads and necks, the ears and cheeks covered with hat flaps fastened under the chin, only our nose being exposed to elements. We wore knee length boots made from the felt, the soles were about one inch thick, with 3/4inch felt covering the foot, and the rest of the boot up to the knee was about ¼ inch thick. The boots had to be one or two sizes too big to allow room for wrapping the feet well. We also wore fur-lined gloves. The only time that we were excused from work was when the temperature dropped to -50c. It happened only once during this particular winter. At lunchtime soup was delivered in a wooden barrel (size of large wine barrel), on a horse drawn sledge driven by a Russian woman. She was selling it with a piece of bread. Often I had no money to pay for this food. My weekly pay was below the subsistence level. For example, if payment for work produced by my gang was, say 1000 roubles, divided equally, each would receive 250 roubles. But it was calculated in the following proportions; I don't remember the actual rates of pay, or the amount of weekly wages, this example is used only to show the disparity in my pay in comparison with the rest of the gang.

Leader 250 x 130% = 325.00

Branch cutter 250 x 105% = 262.50

Branch cutter 250 x 105% = 262.50

Branch burner 250 x 60% = 150.00

I don't know who was responsible for allocation of percentage, was it a

Brigade Leader, the Works Manager, or was the rate fixed for every lumberjack according to the job carried out. The lunch break lasted only about 10-15minutes; it was too cold for malingering.

My job was to collect tree branches and burn them. Carrying armfuls of branches were tearing my clothes; kapok stuffing was coming out from the quilted jacket and trousers. Eventually I began to look like a tramp with my clothes torn to shreds, a walking skeleton covered in boils and carbuncles. I was cold and hungry. I asked a camp commandant for an issue of working clothes, but he said, "The shop is empty and I don't know when the next supply will arrive." The supplies were delivered monthly but nobody knew what and when would be delivered. It could be vodka, tobacco, newspapers, sweets, clothes or perfume, but never all the items at the same time (except for vodka). When anything arrived, there would be a long queue and the shop would be empty in no time. The shopkeeper had the easiest job in the camp. One day, using a ladle to drink water from the wooden barrel in my barrack it tasted of perfume. The men had drunk the perfume and the eau de cologne, instead of giving it to their wives. (Most of the men in the camp were single).

Newspapers were always used for toilet paper, (there was no toilet paper), and to smoke cigarettes, with tobacco rolled up in the newspaper, (there was no cigarette paper, either). The circulation of a particular newspaper depended on the taste of the smokers, not the readers, as large number of Russians in my camp could not read. The tobacco was made from chopped up stalks and from veins of the tobacco leaves. The ordinary cigarette paper was too flimsy to use, but it was not available anyway. During special days, large banners had to be displayed in posiolek. I was forced to write the banners with few of the Russians that could read and write. Eventually Stanisław Zaręba and I became totally blind during the long Siberian night, but we could see well inside the barrack illuminated by the kerosene lamp. The nights, in fact, were quite light, by combination of white snow, moon and stars augmented by the polar lights. The doctor diagnosed that we had a chicken blindness. The chickens can't see after sunset, so they settle on their perches before sundown, woken up by the cockerel at sunrise. We were cured only after eating a piece of liver, which we managed to obtain with great difficulty. I was now so desperate for warm clothes that I left by train for Monastyrok. When I walked in to the Kpt. Organ's office with my ragged clothes, looking like a scarecrow, he looked at me in amazement, and asked, "What happened?" After my explanation, he wrote a note to the Monastyrok camp shop, where I was issued with a new quilted jacket, trousers, and felt boots. After a good meal with my parents, I returned to my work camp. The camp commandant asked to see me; he was very surprised to see my new outfit. After my explanations, he said, looking embarrassed. "You had missed a days work, in accordance with the new law, I was duty bound to report your absence, shortly you will receive summons to appear in Court." Now, with a smile, he said, "It is a shame to ruin your new clothes. From tomorrow, you will work in your gang with an axe."

I suspect that his action was possibly motivated by fear of Kpt. Organ. My pay as a branch cutter had gone up 105%.

The Health and Safety

I was instructed to cut branches on the other side of the tree log, to prevent an injury if the axe slipped. Any accidental injury was considered self-inflicted; it was a punishable offence with no chance for any compensation. Victim had to prove that it was an accident.

Appearance in Court

A few days later, I received a summons to appear in court at Privodino. On the way to court, I showed the summons to Kpt. Organ. He immediately wrote a note and told me to give it to the Judge. In the small court, almost everybody was charged with being either late to work, or absent from work. Sentence for first offence was a deduction of 25% from weekly pay for 6 months and loss of other privileges. Second offence, was one year in prison; third offence was a year in a Gulag. When my name was called, I handed the envelope to the judge. When he read it, he went red in the face, pointed to the door, and said, "Off you go, you lucky fellow." I realized then how powerful the NKVD was. In a Soviet worker's paradise, the pay was so low, because the working targets were impossible to achieve without cheating, so people would rather stay home. To combat absenteeism, the above legislation was introduced to force everybody to work, backed up by a slogan;" If you do not work, you do not eat." On the way back from court, I collected from my father, the hair clippers, cutthroat razor, scissors and comb.

Continuing to Work in Sieviernoje

All the men in the camp needed a haircut; having got the tools, I started practicing haircutting for money, which I needed very much. Now I could afford to buy soup at lunchtime, and to eat in the canteen. Nearly everybody returning from the forest would go to canteen to warm up by drinking three to four glasses of boiled water, kipiatok, which was free of charge, or three or four glasses of tea, which was chargeable, with one boiled sweet, if available. Lumps of sugar were very rare. The sweet would be held in the mouth whilst sipping tea to sweeten the drink.

My brigade gang leader was good at cheating the amount of work we did, which increased my pay, augmented further by income from haircutting. I was no longer starving.

A lumberjacking gang was made up of four men. First, the leader would cut two, or three trees down. Two men, including myself, would cut branches with axes, flush with the tree trunk. The leader then would cut the tree to the required length in accordance with the designated specification. The lengths, ranging from 2m to 5m, could be for musical instruments, railway sleepers, boat building, mine props, firewood, wood for building industry, paper industry, etc. He then proceeded to cut a further two or three trees. The fourth man, (not me now), had to burn branches. At the end of the day, the surveyor would come to measure the lengths of the timber, and stamp the narrow end with the metal stamp imprinting with single letter, denoting designation and diameter in centimeters. The length of each piece had to be cut exactly accurate for designated use, (e.g. 3.20 meters not 3.18 or 3.22). After the surveyor had gone, our gang leader who knew which pieces he cut slightly longer, would cut off the stamped ends and burn them on fire, and resubmit the timber as part of next days work.

At the end of each day, the tree logs had to be stacked up in a pile to be visible after any further snowfall. My next job, was to drag the logs from the forest on the sledge pulled by the horse. I had to load on to the sledge the thick ends of the 3 to 5m logs, (depending on the diameter), with thinner ends dragging in the snow. The logs were dragged out of the forest and stacked up by other men in layers creating a stack 6 feet high. There was a one small advantage with this work, that I rode the horse to and from work. The poor horse was undernourished and very skinny with all the ribs and bones protruding visibly. Riding without the saddle on the bony back was uncomfortable and cold. The horse responded to commands of swear words only.

Drinking and Swearing

Most of the men in the camp were single, with nothing to do, so they were getting drunk and were always swearing, after every word proudly used a different swear word including blasphemous swear words. I was disgusted at their swearing. My gang leader was an exception, a solicitor deported for political offence against the state, he was intelligent and nice to talk to during break for smoke by the fire. The break was always short, because we were getting cold. The only way to keep warm was to keep on working.

One day in the forest, I heard a woman's voice swearing, I went to investigate and came face to face with my school friend, Janina Oleś, swearing at a horse. Both of us were greatly embarrassed. Janina said, "This horse obeys only a string of swear words," I replied, "I know." I was so upset by this incident, that I made myself a promise, that, "I would never swear and never get drunk." I did not want to drop down to their gutter level. I realize that swearing and drinking is a common practice in the Soviet Union, but I am still appalled at this behaviour. I was 18 then, but I kept this promise to this day, I am now 87. My next job, just outside the forest with 3 other men, was to stack up the timber brought on sledges drawn by horses, some driven by women. Pay was equal for the four of us. My next job, with the same 3 men was to load the stacked timber on to the tractors, then to stack them again, next to the railway line. Because we had to wait for the next tractor or train to come, we had a small heated cabin for shelter.

The next hardest work, was to manually load this timber on to the wagons, lifting logs up to 2 meters high. Similar methods of cheating were used. In Siberia, only alcohol thermometers were used, because the mercury would freeze. Tractors and lorries used diesel, but were difficult to start in the morning, without first heating the engines with wood fire below. Petrol could not be used, as it would freeze in those low temperatures. The Polish woodburning locomotive, was the most reliable transport vehicle.

Hygiene

Outside the camp complex, was a sauna bath in the log cabin. Inside was also Voshoboyka, (Lice killer cupboard, heated to a high temperature), where everybody would hang their clothes while using a sauna. The lice and their eggs were killed, but clothes were often damaged. Now I understood why Russians after invading Poland, declared, that Poles were not hygienic, because we had no Voshoboyka in our bathrooms. They could not believe that we really had no problem with lice in Poland.

Wolves

Nadia found out that I was working in the nearby posiołek and written asking me to visit her at her posiołek, 'Station of the Young', 3 miles away. I spoke to the Russian friend who said, "Beware of wolves." I asked, "Are they dangerous?" He replied, "Only when they are hungry. There is no shortage of food for the wolves, if you see them, do not run, and do not fall." Nadia and I met in the canteen and chatted over glass of tea, she informed me that her year in Siberia was nearing the end and she would be returning to Moscow shortly. After saying good-bye to Nadia, I set off on my journey home along the railway line, which was cleared of snow. On each side, there was a forest with about 50ft of clear space on each side of the line. The night was very cold, but illuminated by the moon, stars and the polar lights reflecting in the white snow. It was light enough to read a newspaper. After a while, I heard a howl, looking to the left I noticed a pack of wolves in the shadow of the trees, about 50ft away, following me.

Remembering the advice given, I walked carefully on the frozen slippery railway sleepers, surrounded by an eerie silence; the only sound was the crunch of frozen snow under my feet, and occasional howl of the wolves. Suddenly, I almost jumped out of my skin on hearing a loud noise caused by a tree branch cracked by the frost. I was now really afraid, with a feeling of ants crawling down my spine, but I carefully walked on, keeping my eyes on the wolves, and ahead on the railway sleepers. Lucky for me, just before Sieviernoje, the wolves disappeared; they obviously were not hungry that particular night.

I did not visit Nadia again.

Stalin's Birthday

The Camp Commandant called a meeting in the canteen, announcing that shortly it will be Stalin's birthday. "Workers all over the Soviet Union agreed to work extra 2 hours per day without pay as a present to Stalin. I propose that we work an extra two hours per day for two months without pay. I put this proposal to your vote, who is against it?" One man lifted his hand up. The commandant ignoring the vote against, announced, "The vote for the proposal was unanimous. Start an extra two hours from tomorrow." Next day, the man who voted against, was absent. When I asked one Russian what happened to him, he replied, "Do not ask." None of us were sure if this proposal was really voted on all over the Soviet Union, but it was not safe to ask questions.

Everybody in the Soviet Union was encouraged and rewarded for reporting on fellow workers, even on members of their own Family. Children at school were given commendations and medals for reporting on strangers, their parents, or other members of family.

In our posiołek, was a big strong man called Ivan, working on his own. He managed to exceed daily Stachanov norms. He had eaten well, didn't drink, and didn't smoke, and there was nothing else that he could spend his money on. He kept savings in his pillowcase.

Somebody reported him to NKVD; the money was confiscated, in spite of his explanations that he earned the money honestly, by working hard. NKVD man said, "I don't believe you; nobody in the Soviet Union can save money working honestly," and walked away with the poor man's money. After that experience, Ivan worked slower and spent the money he earned.

Return to my family in Monastyrok

In April 1941, I was transferred back to Monastyrok to be reunited with my family, and of course with the bed bugs.

I discovered to my great sorrow that my youngest sister, Zofia, had died on 24th December 1940, of meningitis.

My brother Ted had broken his leg in October 1940, and was still in Kotlas hospital. Danuta informed me that, "Number of people died in our camp," but good news was that in November 1940, our grandmother Salomea has sent us parcel containing, communion bread, honey, sugar, biscuits and vegetable seeds. Helena said that in the spring she will plant the seeds in the little garden under our window, to provide us with the vegetables, to supply us with so badly needed vitamins."

Certificate of Death for Zofia Mączka, obtained from Moscow, 30 April 2002

Grandmother mentioned that our servants continue to live in our house, but due to very heavy frost in Poland, most of the fruit trees in the orchard had perished. (My father always wrapping the tree trunks with straw to protect from frost).

The food in our posiołek canteen was mainly fish soup, boiled with an odd fish head floating in the water. Another soup, contained few chopped cabbage leaves. Bread rations were issued only to the workers, and to children.

The food supplies brought from Poland finished. Mother exchanged all her jewellery and clothes for food. She discovered one Russian across the river Dvina who was prepared to exchange a sack of potatoes for my father's black wedding suit. Suit was worn only once at his wedding, in 1921. I managed to borrow a small boat, and rowed with mother across the river. The Russian was very pleased with the suit and gratefully gave us the potatoes. When we entered the boat with the sack of potatoes, the boat was taking water with nearly every wave. Mother was scooping the water out, whilst I was rowing this wobbly boat very carefully, constantly in danger of sinking. Rowing this very wide river appeared to be endless, but after crossing the middle, the waves became smaller so we managed to arrive safely.

People in the camp were desperately short of food. I obtained permission from Kpt. Organ to take a group of women to pick mushrooms in the nearby forest.

As an experienced mushroom picker in Poland, I hoped that I would manage to find some here. The forest was like a jungle, with dense undergrowth, large trees and no footpaths. We had to walk over, or round the fallen trees without seeing any mushrooms. The women, after losing sense of direction, began to worry how we will find our way back. I reassured them that I have a very good sense of direction in the forest, and I will bring them back safely.

Soon after, I managed to locate mushrooms; I checked that the baskets were filled only with edible ones. To the surprise and great relief of my party, I led them safely back out of the forest.

I discovered from Danuta's diary that she also made successful mushroom trips.

I started in sawmill, a 12 hour shift work, unloading timber from the wagons arriving from the forest, (12 hours per day for five day week, working 60 hours per week). The days were long, with sun going down at 11.30 pm. rising again by 1am. It was never really dark. When I was thirsty, I would walk down a steep incline through the bushes to the stream to drink water. As soon as I entered the bushes, I was immediately attacked by thousands of mosquitoes covering my face completely. I would slap my face killing hundreds at a time, but even more would come to attack me. Once I got out of the bushes, the mosquitoes would disappear.

Sometime at the end of September 1941, wagons arrived empty from the forest without any timber. The saw mill manager expected thousands of cubic meters more in the forest, but there was none. I was not surprised at all, knowing about the cheating going on in the forest.

One day, I read a book borrowed from the camp library, called Podniataja Celina, (Virgin Soil Upturned), by Sholokhov. The book described a newly created village, populated by ex Soviet soldiers given farmland in equal sized plots for services rendered. Some of the men not keen to cultivate the land had rented it to their neighbours, then spent time drinking and occasionally labouring at one of the farms. After several years, most of the land was owned by a few hardworking farmers, employing most of the previous owners. Then, one early morning in the thirties, came a knock on the door of the newly rich peasants, by NKVD, accompanied by policemen. NKVD man read out an order of deportation to Siberia. The ex soldier asked: "Why?" NKVD replied, "Because now you are a Kulak, a blood sucking capitalist, and an enemy of the State." The ex soldier protested: "It must be a mistake; I am a highly decorated war hero, good, hard working and loyal citizen'. NKVD man replied, "No mistake, all kulaks like you are being deported today."

The book ends with the land distributed equally again.

I read this book with great interest and amazement that it was allowed to be published in the Soviet Union, and available in libraries.

"Good workers punished, lazy and drunkards rewarded "

The hard work and enterprise were not rewarded in the Soviet Union. The Stachanov norm system allowed for earnings to be sufficient only for survival, anybody managing to save was accused of illegal practices or black racketeering. The savings would be confiscated.

Amnesty

Amnesty is a misnomer. We were not sentenced for any crime.

22 June 1941, Hitler attacked the Soviet Union, drove the Red Army out of Poland, and advanced deep into the Soviet Territory.

General Anders and General Sikorski 21 Aug. 1941

30 July 1941, Soviet minister Mayski signed an agreement with General Sikorski the prime minister of the Polish Government in London, agreeing to give Amnesty to Polish Citizens held in the Soviet Union, and to form a Polish Army to fight the Germans under Polish command of General Anders. General Anders was newly released prisoner from Lublianka prison in Moscow. Army Head quarters and a recruitment office were set up in Buzułuk with the Polish flag flying, 500 miles south east from Moscow.

The decree of Amnesty was issued on 12th August 1941, which included return of Polish citizenship, and the right to settle unconditionally in the Soviet Union. (Poland was now occupied by Germans). Thousands of Polish war prisoners were released from Gulags and work camps, posioleks, making their way to join the Polish Army being setup in various camps in the southern regions of the Soviet Union, Uzbekistan and Kazakhstan.

DOWODZTWO
POLSKICH SIŁ ZBROJNYCH
- w r -
Z.S.S.R.

R O Z K A Z   Nr. 1

L. 1/41
Moskwa. Dn. 22.VIII.1941

I. Na mocy umowy Rządu Rzeczypospolitej Polskiej z Rządem
Z.S.S.R. zawartej w Londynie dnia 30 lipca 1941 r.
i umowy wojskowej zawartej przez upełnomocnionych
przedstawicieli obydwóch stron w Moskwie dnia 14 sierp-
nia 1941 r. zostają utworzone suwerenne Polskie Siły
Zbrojne na terenie Z.S.S.R.

II. Rozkazem Naczelnego Wodza W.P. L.4118 z dnia 14.VIII.41
zostałem mianowany Dowódcą Polskich Sił Zbrojnych w
Z.S.S.R.

III. Zadaniem naszym jest wspólna z wojskami Z.S.S.R., Wiel-
kiej Brytanii i innych sojuszników walka aż do osta-
tecznego zwycięstwa przeciwko odwiecznemu naszemu wro-
gowi - Niemcom.

IV. Wzywam wszystkich obywateli R.P., zdolnych do noszenia
broni, by spełnili swój obowiązek względem Ojczyzny i
wstąpili pod sztandary Orła Białego.

Pamiętajcie, że zwycięstwo Niemiec - to nie tylko
bezpowrotna zguba Polski, lecz również całkowita za-
głada Narodu Polskiego.

Dowódca Polskich Sił Zbrojnych
w Z.S.S.R.

Władysław   A n d e r s
generał dywizji

First Order by General Anders issued 22nd Aug. 1941

Translation by Stefan Mączka follows:

ORDER Nr. 1

In accordance with the agreement between Governments of Poland and USSR in London 30 July 1941, and military agreement in Moscow 14 August 1941, began sovereign Polish Armed Forces in USSR.

By order of the Commander-in-chief of the Polish Armed Forces, I was appointed

Commander of Polish Armed Forces in USSR.

Our object is joint with army of USSR., Great Britain and other allies in fight to achieve ultimate victory against our eternal enemy, Germany.

I call all Polish citizens able to carry arms, to carry out their duty to our country, and enlist to serve under the standard of White Eagle. Remember, that German victory would be not only the loss of Poland forever, but also complete annihilation of Polish Nation.

Unfortunately, very few people were released from our camp, mostly the older men, but nobody of military age. From Monastyrok, the first group had been released on 5th September; second group on 18th October, including other nearby posioleks.

A number of 18 to 25 year old young men, including myself, pleaded with Kpt. Organ for release papers. Kpt. Organ, each time discouraged us in an apparently false fatherly caring voice, "Boys, it is in your own interest to stay and work in this camp. What would you do with yourself if I gave you a pass allowing you to travel in Soviet Union, without money, not knowing where to go? Without this document you will not receive soup and bread rations at railway stations."

We firmly believed that Kpt. Organ wanted to keep us on his work force, so he could achieve his production targets, as most of the local Russian workers were conscripted to the Soviet Army.

We were afraid that not being able to join the Polish Army, we would remain in Siberia forever.

One day, there was no bread delivery. The sawmill manager said he could not do anything about bread. My father said, "We are hungry we don't have strength to work, we will go on strike unless we receive the bread." The manager said: "Strikes are against the law in the Soviet Union, unless you resume work immediately I will report you to NKVD." Kpt. Organ was astonished; he was never in that situation before, my father, as a spokesman, stated firmly, "We are not afraid of any threats; we will not work until we receive bread." To our great surprise, Kpt. Organ made a promise: "Return to work, I will ensure that bread is delivered within one and half hours." He kept his promise, demonstrating again the power of NKVD.

His hand had been weakened, because all Russian workers were conscripted to serve in the Russian Army.

CHAPTER FIVE

ESCAPE FROM SIBERIA 14 NOVEMBER 1941

Weeks go by. Nobody is released from our posiołek. It was now 12th November 1941, and whispers started circulating, that there will be no more transports from Kotlas railway station. My young friends and I, being very worried, arranged a meeting that evening.

We decided to find out what was happening at Kotlas station.

I volunteered with Gienek Nowak to do just that.

We packed a small rucksack with provisions, and in the morning, as usual, we reported for work at sawmill.

The control of attendance in the mornings was stricter than in the afternoons. At noon, after whistle for lunch break, we carefully slipped out from the sawmill to walk 16 miles to Kotlas. We walked through snow 2ft deep, following the track made by sledges and lorries. Finally, we could see the town on top of the hill, but first, we had to cross the frozen river Dvina.

We noticed in front of us, a group of prisoners cutting the ice blocks from the river, guarded by soldiers. We stopped to consider what to do. One option, was to divert from the road and walk through 2ft deep snow. It would be hard work going through this virgin snow, but also it would draw the attention of the soldiers. So we decided to brave it out, and to carry on walking. One of the soldiers stepped forward, lowered his rifle with the bayonet, and called out; "Stop, where are you going," I answered in my perfect Siberian Russian: "To join the Red Army, to fight Germans." The soldier then said, "Documents." We both felt frozen with fright, we had no documents, but went through the motions of searching our pockets. My friend produced a piece of paper, which the soldier grabbed very quickly. Noticing that he was examining it upside down, I gave him my piece of paper, which he returned, and stepped aside to let us go!

We were extremely lucky that he could not read, as this was only a pass with an official stamp allowing us to walk over the railway bridge, only when we were unloading wagons.

Kotlas station was very crowded, with many passenger and cattle trains in the sidings. We managed to locate a cattle train with Polish ex deportees in it. They assured us, that this was not the last train for those wishing to join the Polish army.

Their train was now standing in the sidings for two days; nobody knew when it would depart.

We returned to Monastyrok in the evening, and held the meeting with our friends. We decided to escape the next day. I informed my father. He said, "I also was a volunteer in 1918. I am not going to try to stop you. Good luck, and God bless you, my son." Seven of us packed a rucksack each, reported for work in the morning of 14th November 1941, and at noon, we managed to slip out un-observed, and set off for Kotlas.

		Age
1	Biedul Jerzy	16
2	Mączka Stefan Bogusław	18
3	Morawski Wojtek	17
4	Nowicki Tadeusz	18
5	Nowak Eugeniusz (Gienek)	17
6	Oleś Kazik	17
7	Zaręba Stanisław	17

Without obstacles on the way, we managed to locate the same Polish cattle train in the sidings. After finding a wagon with enough room for us, we sat on the top bunk, opened a bottle of vodka to celebrate our lucky escape. Suddenly, we heard a voice of our NKVD commandant calling our names, in the next wagon. Quickly, we hid amongst luggage under the bottom bunk. Kpt. Organ came to our coach with two local policemen, called out all our names, and then said, "They are not here, let's check the next wagon." Half an hour later, at 4.30pm, 14thNovember 1941, our train departed. Our journey into the unknown had begun.

I gave many talks in England about my Siberian experiences since 1974. I always said that we were extremely lucky that Kpt. Organ had not seen us, or we would have been sent to a Gulag.

In 1981, I found Ted Nowicki in a nursing home near York. Whilst recollecting our escape, I said how lucky we were that Kpt. Organ has not seen us. Ted replied; "He did see me and Stanislaw Zaręba. There was no room for us to hide with you, so we just stood frozen stiff with fright. Kpt. called all our names whilst looking intensely at both of us, then said, they are not here, let's check the next wagon."

I said to Ted, "Good job you did not panic, otherwise we would have been arrested." Ted replied, "I was in a panic; I just could not move or speak with fright."

This was a further and final proof, that Kpt. Organ was an exceptional, and humane NKVD individual.

The local policemen with him did not know us, but even so, Kpt. Organ had taken a great risk. If he was reported, he would have been shot, and the person reporting him would have received a medal. Not all deportees from Monastyrok would agree. They considered Captain Organ to be a very severe, and ruthless officer.

NKVD controlled all aspects of Soviet life, controlled all the Gulags and work camps in the Soviet Union, numbering at that time, approx. 20 million people. This cheap, slave labour, was used for work in the forest, building roads, railways and bridges, and canals, including Leningrad-Moscow Canal, coalmines and the deadly lead mines, and many other large projects. NKVD was responsible only to Beria, the head of the NKVD, who in turn was responsible only to Stalin.

The Polish army recruiting camps were being set up in southern Russia, thousands of miles apart, nobody had any idea where our train was going. But we did not worry about that, we were happy to be free.

Our train was always stopping at bigger stations, shunted into sidings for a day or two, to allow passenger and military traffic to pass. During one of the stops, we changed wagons, to join four young girls and seven men, mostly middle aged, increasing the numbers in the new wagon to 18.

Ted Nowicki played a mandolin; all of us were singing, we were now so happy. We could buy soup at bigger stations, but the queue was always long. The men in our wagon took in turns to stand in the queue with the bucket for soup, with another man queuing with a large jug for boiled water (Kipiatok). One young man in our wagon called Nowak, not Eugeniusz Nowak, I will refer to him as John, volunteered to buy soup. He was wearing a greatcoat and hat similar to the Red Army uniform.

He pushed his way to the head of the queue by calling out; "Give way to a soldier," it worked for him. When it was my turn at Perm station, I borrowed his coat, but unfortunately, the Red Army soldiers were standing by, so I dared not push my way to the head of the queue. After collecting the soup, I found that the train had left the station, this was most unusual, as cattle trains had normally low priority so were shunted in the sidings for a day or two, or longer.

I was greatly disappointed and worried, what could I do?

I managed, illegally, to board a passenger train, hoping that it would travel in the same direction. I had no ticket, no documents, but luckily, I was not asked for any, maybe I was mistaken for a soldier wearing John's army coat.

Two days later, after crossing the Ural Mountains, the train stopped at Sverdlovsk (now Yekaterinburg), a large city and a main rail junction. I set off to look for my cattle train in the sidings, there were dozens of cattle and passenger trains standing, full of the Russians fleeing east. After about one hour, I located my wagon.

Imagine how surprised and pleased everybody was to see me with the bucket of cold soup, and specially Nowak to have his coat back.

The soup was heated on the stove, and after two days in the sidings, we continued with our journey.

So far, we travelled for 19 days from Kotlas, via Kirov and Perm.

On the 3rd of December, our train took a southern route from Sverdlovsk, along the eastern side of the Ural Mountains, via Chelyabinsk and Orsk. Please consult the following map on next page.

Journey to find the Polish Army

1. Black Line at the top Deportation from Równe to Kotlas

2. Escape from Kotlas

Below: Extracted from Document confirming deportation of my family to Siberia, 10 February 1940, arriving 29th February 1940.

Moscow 3 January 2002.

Polish Commission Association Memorial 103051 Moscow, Malyi Karetnyi Pereulok, 12. In the archive records (BD) Polish deportees (Spiecpieriesieleńcy) in Arkhangelsk region in 1940-1941.

Extracted by employees of archives of the Ministry of Interior (USW) of the Arkhangelsk region in accordance with agreement with the Centre of Research and Information (OBIU) Memorial in Moscow, compiled from the personal records in the files of deported persons in 1940 to Arkhangelsk region from western region of Ukrainian SRR and from Belarus SRR.

Verified initially by the OBIU Memorial there is the following information about Zofja Mączka and 5 members of her family:

1. Mączka Stefan Antonowicz (Stefan son of Anthony) Born 1895

2. Mączka Helena Stefanowna (daughter of Stefan) Born 1905

3. Mączka Stefan Stefanowicz (son of Stefan) Born 1922

4. Mączka Danuta Stefanowna (daughter of Stefan) Born 1925

5. Mączka Zofja Stefanowna (daughter of Stefan) Born 1926

Zofja died 24/12/1940

6. Mączka Tadeusz Stefanowicz (Son of Stefan) Born 1927

Whole family is shown as born in Tuczyn, region of Równe, social category Osadnik (military settler), arrived 29 February to Specposiolek Monastyrok, near the town of Kotłas in the Archangel Region. In the Archives of USW Arkhangelsk Region, there is also a list of persons released from Settlements (Specposiołków) per amnesty for Polish citizens, declared 12 September 1941 by decree of the Presidium Highest Council ZSRR. In this list are shown only two members of Zofia family.

1. Mączka Stefan, son of Antoni, born 1895 w Korotkowie in Kielce region, domiciled in Tuczyn, Równe region, farmer, after release (from deportation) went to Uzbek SRR.

2. Mączka Stefan, son of Stefan, born 1922 in Aleksandria region, domiciled in Tuczyn in Równe region, student, escaped 14/11/1941.

In the documents in the archives there is official name of Specposiołek as Monastyrok (situated 3 km from village Priwodino, 7 km from railway halt Nowinki and 22 km from the railway station Kotłas), also on some registry cards appears a name Monastyrskaja, or Monastyrskij, (According to the official terminology, these were not a labour camps, but special settlement. The difference is based on the fact that corrective labour camps (also called Gulags) were reserved for people sentenced to loss of liberty, while specialposiołek (special settlements) were for deportees, people without a court hearing, for whom was arranged a different kind of repression-namely restriction of liberty) (special settlement=free labour, as opposed to penal settlement/ labour)

One more clarification: Privodino and Nowinki are situated by the river Siewiernaja Dwina, not Wyczegda.

With feeling of personal moral responsibility as citizen of my country, which was guilty against Poland and Poles, please accept my expression of sorrow and sympathy connected with the premature death of Zofja Mączka and sorrow for suffering and wrong experienced by her and other members of her family.

With respect.

Aleksander Gurjanow.

Member of the Polish Commission.

Translated 22 February 2004 by Stefan Bogusław Mączka.

Corrections below by Stefan Bogusław Mączka:

It is incorrect that the whole Maczka family was born in Tuczyn.

1. Mączka, Stefan. Born 1895 in Gowarczów Kielce region.

2. Mączka, Helena. Born 1905 in Witkowice nr.Kraków.

3. Mączka, Stefan. Born 1922 at Osada Krechowiecka.

4. Mączka, Danuta. Born 1925 at Osada Krechowiecka.

5. Mączka, Zofja. Born 1926 at Osada Krechowiecka.

6. Mączka, Tadeusz. Born 1927 in Kraków.

On 19th December, we arrived at Aral Town by the Aral Sea. We were now in a warmer area, no more snow, so we started exchanging our winter clothes for food.

My friend, Gienek, with whom we scouted Kotlas, had a new shirt, hoping to exchange it for food. Nobody in the street was interested, we knocked at the door of a small house, we went in and explained our predicament, but no luck. On the way out, my friend spotted on the shelf in the corridor a small bag of flour, about 20lbs. He wrapped it in his new shirt, and walked out. I tried to persuade him to give it back, "They are poor people and we should never steal personal possessions." He replied, "It is for the benefit of our wagon." In fact, we always shared food with everybody in our wagon.

Without warm clothes, I was cold in the night, so I moved two timber planks across the wagon placing them above the stove. I slept like this for the rest of the journey. We were now completely infested by body lice in our hair and our clothes, we felt terrible, with no way of getting rid of them. The lice and their eggs were located mostly in the shirt seams, I tried to burn lice and eggs against the hot stove and partly succeeded, but after putting the shirt on, the sleeves came off. With cotton threads burned, I ended up with a sleeveless shirt. This was my one and only shirt, all my spare clothes were exchanged for food. On 24th December, Ted exchanged his mandolin for food. He managed to get only soup and a couple of loaves of bread. This meagre food stopped us from being totally hungry, but what a sad Christmas it was for us. We passed Tashkent and Samarkand. At Bukhara, I managed to exchange my barber tools for a loaf of bread from a woman shopper, who said that I spoke Russian with a Siberian accent. Each of us in the wagon had just a slice of bread. We were hungry and depressed, even beginning to regret our escape. Maybe we should have listened to Kpt. Organ's advice, and waited for the release papers. By now, we exchanged all our possessions for food; even rucksacks, except for an old one, which nobody wanted. We had nothing other than the clothes we were wearing, which were in a very shabby state. I am sure nobody in their right mind would give anything for those rags. We were hungry, dirty, unwashed, overrun by body lice.

In spite of the condition we were in, nobody in our wagon complained or despaired about our situation, we just looked forward to joining the Polish Army.

Next day, the 5th of January 1942, after travelling for 51 days, we arrived at our destination town called Guzar, in Uzbekistan, near the Caspian Sea and Persian and Afghanistan borders.

At Guzar station, the Russian officials informed us that, "The Polish Army would start recruitment here in about four weeks time. In the meantime you would be directed to villages where you will have to work without pay for your keep."

Eighteen people from our wagon were directed to an Uzbek village, 30 km (19miles) away. We were dreading such a long walk; we were tired, weakened by lack of food, not having eaten for the last 24 hours. No food was offered by the Russians in Guzar.

We were told, "On your arrival in the village, you will receive food."

After a few miles walk we noticed a small village near the road, Ted and I walked over to ask for some food. One Uzbek produced a large knife and said, "On your way, you tramps." We certainly looked like tramps.

Uzbek Collective Farm

After great effort, I do not know how we managed to arrive at our destination, we were directed to a compound with buildings constructed from clay mixed with straw. The three buildings were linked by high walls.

Each of us received a small dish filled with something that looked like milky oats porridge. After tasting it, I spat it out in disgust. It tasted horrible, for me, it was inedible. Uzbeks explained that it was oats with a fermented mare's milk, considered by them to be a delicacy. I was starving, but I just could not force myself to eat it. It was explained to us that we would have to work on a Collective Cotton Farm without pay, but we will receive daily food rations, starting from this evening.

We were shown to our quarters, a mud hut in this quadrangle. There was no electricity, no running water, no toilet, and no washing facilities. None of us had a bath, or proper wash since 14th November, 1941.The hut was about 15ft x 20ft long.

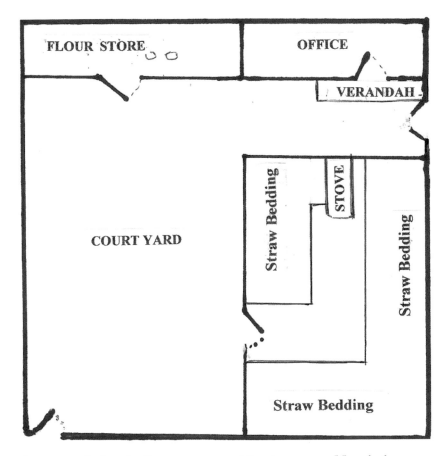

Accommodation for four women and fourteen men. No windows, beds, chairs, table no water, no toilet.

The earth floor on each side of the wall was covered with straw and large camel blankets. At the end of the room, was a fireplace for cooking. Utensils were placed on the oven and little low table beside it. The four girls chose to sleep near the door. We were very hungry; we were by now at the desperate survival level. It is said that sex is the strongest driving force in life, but not for us. We were now reduced down to the most basic animal instinct, "The survival." None of us boys and girls even gave a thought to sex.

Our rations arrived. One cup of flour, about 7 ounces per person, and piece of lamb, equivalent to about two oxo cubes each. We protested that these rations were insufficient. The Uzbek man replied, "We didn't want you.

NKVD ordered us to take you in. If you don't like it, then you are free to go."

The girls decided to cook a soup, and to make some sort of bread from the rest of the flour. We enjoyed this simple meal, but it was not enough to satisfy our hunger, and we had to save some of the soup and bread for the next day. Next morning, we were issued with tools, taken to the field where the cotton had been harvested, we had to dig out the roots of the cotton plants. The soil was dry and very hard, not easy to dig. We were used to very hard work, but now being weakened by lack of food, it was an almost impossible task. The morning was very misty, a flock of sheep passed by, followed by a shepherd riding a donkey. Ted remarked, "If only we could catch one of the sheep it would keep us going for a few days." I said, "It would be stealing." Ted said, "This is a collective, not personal farm, and we are desperate for food. The Uzbeks gave us insufficient rations as payment for our work." I replied, "In that case, we should try."

We made our way to the water canal used for irrigation of the cotton fields. In the narrow access to the water, the sheep were drinking, one or two at a time, no sign of the shepherd. We tried in vain a number of times, but eventually, we managed to catch one of the smaller sheep by its horns. At our farm in Poland, I watched my father kill a sheep, pig and calves, but I only knew how to kill a chicken by chopping its head off with an axe. Now I only had a penknife. We dragged the sheep inside the dry canal, I asked Ted to keep a lookout, whilst I tried to kill this animal with my small penknife with 2.5 inch blade. The sheep was making a loud noise, so I clamped his mouth with my left hand, whilst cutting his throat with my right hand. I couldn't cut through bones of the neck, so I twisted and turned the head round until the neck bones broke and the head came off. I hid the head under dry grass in the canal. Ted and I got hold of its front legs, and were dragging it along, when we noticed that fog was thinning and the village was becoming visible. We looked for cover. Having spotted some sort of an enclosure surrounded by a hedge, we went in, and suddenly we were confronted by a big bull. We were warned that the bull was dangerous, so we ran away, dragging the sheep behind us. When I turned round, I could see the bull eating grass, obviously not interested in us. What a relief! We found a small bushy area 3 ft high, with a little clearing amongst the prickly bushes. I said, "Ted, keep a look-out whilst I skin the sheep." Suddenly, Ted called out, "Shepherd." We both laid down, the shepherd passed very close by on his donkey, luckily not looking down our way. After that, we hid the sheep under the bush and joined our work party. In the evening, we were issued with the day's rations. Our protest about small portions was again ignored.

After dark, we returned to collect the sheep with a bucket, an axe and a sharp kitchen knife. We cut the sheep into pieces and carried it back in the bucket. That night we had a little feast, but we were short of flour. One of the friends volunteered to make a key for the padlock of the storeroom of this collective farm. Ted and I, volunteered to get the flour. The store was located next to a village office, always with the lights on, somebody inside was working most nights. Ted and I, decided to brave it. After midnight, Ted opened the padlock and the door. After I went in, Ted put the padlock back on and lay down on the ground below the doorstep. In the faint light from the moon filtering through the window, I spotted a very big camel sack. I scooped about 20lbs of flour in to the old rucksack, the one nobody wanted, without noticeable dimunition of the flour in the sack. I knocked on the door for Ted to let me out; I would hurry back to our room, whilst Ted shut the door, and replaced the padlock.

Ted and I decided to ration the food, and we informed the group accordingly, in addition to our insufficient daily rations, because we did not know when the extra food would come. There were no objections to this proposal. We knew that if we took too much flour it would draw the attention of Uzbeks, and this source of supply would stop. Our daily ration of flour was: one cupful of 7 ounces per person (18 persons x 7 ounces = 126 ounces = about 8lbs. Flour stolen from store about 20 lbs, was intended to last for at least 3 days, allowing each person extra one cup of flower to supplement their official daily ration.

One night, I filled the rucksack with flour and knocked on the door once, signalling Ted to let me out, he knocked twice with an agreed signal for me to stay put and wait. I waited with trepidation, seemingly for ages, when suddenly Ted let me out. When we got back I asked him; "What happened?" Ted replied, "An Uzbek came out of the office, only 30 feet from where I lay below the door, standing on the top step he started peeing, looking around before going back inside."

This incident made us realize even more, how risky it was to steal this flour. Next night, one of the boys in our group, discretion forbids me to name him, had insisted that the portions should be increased, or he will report us to Uzbeks. In reply, I said to Ted; "Give him the key so he can take the next turn to bring flour." The 17-year-old boy would not take the key, and just started to cry. This incident, illustrates the level of self-preservation for survival, reached by this boy.

It was remarkable that nobody else in our group complained, the four girls aged about 18, did not cry either. Three days, Ted and I got more flour, but we were now without meat, there was no sheep around. Lots of food was needed to feed 18 under-nourished people. John Nowak, suggested that we could try to kill a piglet in the village. Ted and I refused to take part, "Let somebody else take the risk." As nobody was willing, Ted said to John, "I will go with you." After midnight, they set off with an axe and a sack, shortly after, we were suddenly woken up by the pig's scream, and all the village dogs barking. Soon after that, our two boys rushed in and got under the covers, two Uzbek men followed. They looked around and noticed Ted's wet felt boots protruding from under the cover. "Where have you been?" Ted replied, "To the toilet." After a while, they left. It turned out that John hit a piglet on its head with a glancing blow; the pig fell down, and screamed. John hit the pig again, hard on the head. Ted put the pig in the sack and they both ran. Ted dropped the sack with the pig in the ditch. Very early next morning, Ted collected the pig from the ditch, and the meat, with careful rationing, lasted for about five days. As nobody else would take a turn to steal the flour, Ted and I continued to carry on this risky operation. Three weeks went by, we recovered partly from hunger, but there were no more sheep in sight, and pigs were too risky. Quite unexpectedly, our youngest companion, Jerzy Biedul turned up with two chickens and six eggs. He raided a collective chicken house, and wrung the necks of chickens, without waking up the village. John and I set off for Guzar to find out about the Polish Army. The recruiting office was being set up with the Polish flag flying on the building, but actual recruiting would start on the 5th February 1942. Next day, we returned to the village to give good news to our friends. For the next few days we sustained ourselves with flour supplied by Ted and I, by now we considered that it was our duty. Jerzy Biedul continued to supply us with chickens. This young boy was fearless, he just could not see the danger, and we were restraining him from taking too many risks by raiding the chicken house. He was also willing to take a turn getting flour, but we would not let him. We worked on cotton fields for five days, with one-day rest every week. We had not succeeded in developing any relationship with the villagers, they just ignored us.

We were pleased to leave the village on 4th February. Walking the 19 miles to Guzar was easier this time. By supplementing our rations, we were in better physical condition than a month ago.

The Polish Army in Guzar.

Most of the recruits looked like those two or even worse.

We spent the night in the queue to join the army with many very emaciated ex-Gulag Poles. In the morning, a number of men died, killed by starvation and unexpected frost during the night.

In the queue to the recruitment office, we said good-bye to each of our group of eighteen.

Two professors, old to us, aged about 50-55, with tears in their eyes thanked Ted, John Nowak, Biedul and I for saving their lives.

Out of 14 men, only four were prepared to take a risk. I know that it was, and it is wrong to steal, but I am pleased that we were able to save the lives of 18 people by supplementing their daily rations. Looking back, I now feel rather proud of this achievement.

I never again met any of the seventeen companions from the wagon.

5th February 1942, I enlisted in the Artillery Regiment, billeted in the tents on the high ground in Guzar, overlooking the road.

With shortage of food and medicines, typhus epidemic swept our camp. Each morning, I observed two or three open top lorries with dead bodies wrapped in sheets, loaded like sardines, about 120 bodies a day. The last thing I remember before waking up in hospital, was helping to carry two dead bodies out of my tent.

I was lying on the marble floor covered by straw and blankets in the mosque used as an army field hospital.

Next to me was a piece of bread and a dead body. I lost consciousness again without eating the bread. Next time, I don't know when, I woke up hearing two doctors remarking about my dry skin. I was trying to eat my bread ration, but I could not. The man next to me, asked if he could have my bread. I said, "Yes." Next time I woke up, I thought that I was dreaming, seeing my father looking down on me with a smile on his face, with food in his hands. I thought that it was a miracle.

I do not know how long I had been in this hospital. My father was visiting me daily with food.

My father, with his family, was the last one to be released from Monastyrok. They travelled by cattle train from 2nd January, arrived in Guzar on 22nd February 1942. Considering that number of Polish recruitment camps were situated in Kazakhstan and Uzbekistan, few hundred miles apart from one another, it was a miracle that my father arrived at my camp, and found me. I was very lucky.

One day, I was released from hospital with another man. We were so weak that we walked slowly and with great difficulty, supporting one another and frequently sitting down to rest. My father, on his usual visit helped us up, and walking between us, supported us until we arrived in the camp where we were placed in the quarantine tent.

I continued to be unwell, so I do not remember anything about the quarantine or, how long I was there.

I lost all my personal papers and photographs in the hospital.

Extract from Danuta's diary: *By 1st December 1941, only six families including ours remained in Monastyrok. Danuta was not working so her bread ration was reduced to 100 grams per day. The Christmas was very sad; we had only a few pieces of dry bread to eat. On 27th December 1941 Kpt. Organ at last gave us our release paper, dated 26th December. We left the next day for Kotlas by horse drawn sledge, collected Ted from the hospital on our way to the rail station. In the Kotlas canteen, we were given (for the four of us) 400 grams of bread and soup (which was noted on the back of the permit).*

2nd of January 1942, the train departed in to the unknown direction. 13th February in Tashkent father with three other men had gone to get bread, the train departed without them. 17th February in Andiezan, we found father. We arrived at Guzar on 22nd February 1942. I joined the Polish Women Auxiliary Service on 25th February by giving my age as 18. (I was almost 16 at that time).

What a coincidence that my family's journey from Kotlas to Guzar took 51 days, and our own journey also took 51 days.

Extract from General Anders' book, Without Last Chapter: *All Polish recruitment camps were flooded by volunteers to join the army, including women with children and old people. Soviets supplied us with rations barely sufficient for the soldiers, but no medicines and no uniforms. General Anders issued orders, that food must be shared with our civilians, but diluted rations were not sufficient to sustain life. Typhus, Typhoid and other illnesses were killing people like flies.* General Anders appealed for help directly to Stalin, who replied, "I will continue to supply food for soldiers only, but not for the civilians." In December 1941, General Sikorski, after discussion with the British Government, arrived in Moscow with General Anders to sort out the problems with Stalin. In the meantime, General Anders contacted British ambassador in Tehran for help with transfer of the Polish army and civilians from the Soviet Union to Persia. Stalin, and the British Government had agreed to transfer Polish army to Persia (Now Iran). General Anders was told: "No Jews, and no civilians." British objections against civilians were based on lack of accommodation, food and other supplies in Persia. British were also worried that Jews would escape in Palestine to join the Jewish terrorist organizations.

The Agreement was signed by Stalin and Sikorski, 4th December 1941

General Anders insisted that Jews with Polish citizenship were welcome in the Polish army. General Anders also insisted to include in evacuation all civilians; otherwise, all of them would die.

General Anders was concerned that so few Polish Officers were joining the army, what happened to 11,000 officers held in Kozielsk and Ostaszkov? No satisfactory answer received from Soviets to direct question to Stalin from General Sikorski, "What happened to the Polish officers?" Stalin replied; "Most probably they escaped to Manchuria." Can anyone imagine a bigger and blatant lie than this?

Eventually, General Anders succeeded in persuading Stalin to agree to evacuation of 40,000 soldiers, plus civilians to Persia.

The first train transports started 24th March to Krasnovodsk, a port at the Caspian Sea. Assortment of small ships was scheduled to be ready to depart from 27th March. In this first evacuation, General Anders succeeded in getting out of Russia 43,800 people, (33,000 soldiers and 10,800 civilians). Second, and last evacuation of 44,800 soldiers and 25,500 civilians including a great number of orphans, took place in August 1942. Total 114,100 evacuated out of Soviet Union was only fraction of 1.5 million originally deported to Siberia by Stalin.

Unfortunately, we left behind about 3,200 dead soldiers buried in about 15 Polish cemeteries in Uzbekistan, in addition, many thousands of dead civilians, women and children. There is a record only of soldiers who enlisted and died in the army camps. There is no record of thousands who died on the way to the recruitment camps, neither any record of women and children who died on the way, or, near the recruitment camps.

Guzar (Gazer) with 663 graves. One of 13 restored Polish military cemeteries in Uzbekistan Photo June 2007

Boats and ships overcrowded with Polish soldiers and their families.

The NKVD, on orders from Stalin, efficiently conducted the evacuation to Persia. NKVD warned Poles not to talk about life and conditions in the Soviet Union.

In Krasnovodsk, 29th March, I boarded one of the very crowded assortments of small ships, most of them were not passenger, but commercial ships, such as oil tankers and even larger fishing boats. Father, Helena and Ted, also travelled to Pahlavi, as family of soldiers, including Danuta and I.

It took two days to cross the Caspian Sea to Pahlevi in Persia. Sea was very rough, most of the people were sea sick, number of them died.

Dead were just dropped overboard. There were no toilet facilities, most of the people relieving themselves overboard.

On top deck of one the ships, *helpful* Soviets build a wooden toilet hanging on the side of the ship. Two doors marked Men and Women, but without internal partition between male and female compartments, as remembered by my friend M. Kuczyński. But there was no such a luxury on my ship.

Map of the Middle East 1942/43 and my further travels.

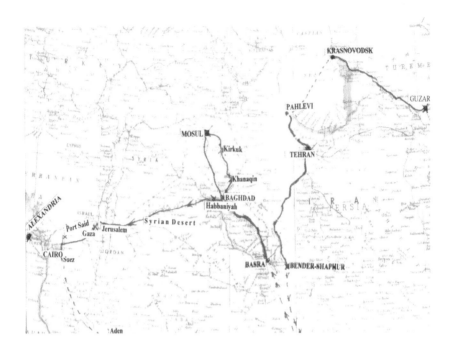

We disembarked at Persian Port of Pahlevi at midnight, 31st March 1942

I remember clearly as if it was yesterday, marching through the streets of Pahlevi, looking in amazement almost unbelieving, at the shops full of food, white bread, cakes, butchers and delicatessen shops full of all the goodies we had not seen since Poland.

We arrived on the beach; it was warm so we slept on the sand. Next morning the 1st of April, British troops arrived with a field kitchen. We were served sandwiches, white bread with cheese and jam, or marmalade followed by dates and tea with milk. It tasted delicious. After breakfast we queued to the big tent in which we stripped naked, all of our body hair was shaved, disinfected, followed by our first shower bath since 13 November 1941. Our old clothes were placed in the big heap on the sand, and were burned. Before leaving the tent, we were issued with new underwear and British summer uniforms. It was wonderful to be clean, free of the Russian body lice. Freedom at last.

After that, we were loaded onto lorries, about twenty per lorry. There were no seats; we had to stand all the way to Tehran. Persian civilian drivers were driving fast on the winding mountain roads, we were holding on to the sides of the lorry for our dear life.

On arrival, we were placed in tents erected in the school playground, right in the centre of Tehran. This was a lovely city, most public buildings gleaming with walls covered with colourful mosaics. Clean streets with water running in the gutters discharged from a number of big houses on both sides of the street lined with trees.

Walking with my friend admiring the sights, we found a gate slightly ajar; we entered a lovely garden with a number of beautiful women, in and around the swimming pool. Suddenly two eunuchs appeared shouting, and waving scimitars, running towards us. The women started laughing. Not being in laughing mood, we escaped safely on to the street. After two weeks recuperation and building our strength, during which time we had to be careful not to eat too much food, our starved, shrunken stomachs had to get used to plentiful, and rich food.

My family was now separated. Father joined the army, and was assigned to the ship to escort German prisoners to South Africa, Canada and Scotland. Mother remained in Tehran to look after Ted, who was in hospital awaiting operation on his leg. Later on in Palestine, I received news that my mother was very ill with typhus in Tehran Hospital.

Photo July 2013. In South Teheran, there is a Dulab cemetery with 3000 Polish graves of emaciated Polish soldiers, women and children who died in hospital and camps in Tehran, in 1942.

Too ill, without a chance to enjoy the freedom after escape from the Soviet workers paradise, I noticed that none of the evacuees from the Soviet paradise were fat. I considered myself very lucky to have recovered from typhus and got out of Russia. Otherwise, I could have been amongst the 3100 that died in Polish Recruitment camps in Kazakhstan and Uzbekistan (including 681 at Guzar) killed mainly by typhus and starvation during 1941-1943. In addition to above recorded 3,100 deaths, there were many more unknown thousands of those who died before reaching the recruitment camps. And, additional hundreds of thousands were left behind in USSR.

Extract from Danuta's Dairy: *I began nursing training course run by the Polish Red Cross in the camp Nr. 4 in Tehran. Unfortunately, on 18Th May 1942, I became ill with Typhus. After release from hospital on 1st August, I returned to camp Nr. 4 for convalescence. I considered myself very lucky that there was a good medical care and medicines available.*

In October 1942, I was transferred to Iraq to join a female transport company in Quizil Rabat.

I heard that Ted Nowicki was sent to England, as part of 3,500 young men to join the Polish Air force, and that Stanislaw Zaręba had died in Guzar Hospital.

Most of the women with children, were transferred by the British to special camps in India, and in various countries of East Africa.

CHAPTER SIX

MILITARY TRAINING IN THE MIDDLE EAST

After one week in Tehran, I was transferred with my unit by rail to a camp about 200 miles south from Tehran for a rest, before journey to Palestine.

I sailed with my unit on an Indian ship from the Persian port of Bandar Shahpur, very near to Basra in Persian Gulf, stopping at Aden port in the Red Sea, Suez Canal to Suez, and by train to Palestine.

But we were not allowed ashore. We had to stay on the ship.

Palestine

We travelled from Suez by train to camp Beit Jirja, 8 miles from Gaza. We were billeted in tents, close to the Mediterranean Sea near the road leading from Gaza to Tel-Aviv.

3 May 1942 in Quastina the 9th and 10th Divisions (of which I was a member) newly arrived from USSR were amalgamated with the 3rd Carpathian Brigade, which recently arrived from Libya after victory at Tobruk, to form: the 3rdCarpathian Rifle Division (3 DSK.).

Soldiers Pay Book

Below: My CO. Col. L. Przybytko.

I was assigned to the 9th battery of the 3rd Carpathian Anti-aircraft Artillery Regiment. The Anti-aircraft regiment had 27 guns divided into 9 batteries of 3 guns each. Training started, pleasantly interrupted by an occasional swim in the Mediterranean Sea.

28 July 1942, I was standing with my back to the road observing a company of soldiers training. Next, I woke up sitting in the car. I asked the Arab driver, "What am I doing here"? He replied; "Have a look down." I looked down and I could see just below the belt, my stomach open and bleeding, I instinctively grabbed the wound with the fingers of my two hands, trying to close the opening, then I fainted. Coming round, I found myself on the operating table, as I was given only a local anaesthetic. I could feel without pain, the doctors' scalpel cutting away edges of the wound, which were dirty with road grit and sand, subsequently inserting 22 stitches.

To this day, I don't know how I was injured, but I have a 9-inch scar to prove it.

30 July, I discharged myself from the hospital. I was so keen to return to my battery unit.

Assembling the gun to the firing position involved lifting some heavy parts, my wound opened up and I ended up in hospital for a further 3 weeks.

Rehovod Hospital Palestine 25th Sept 1942 I am in the middle next to the pretty nurse.

There was no end to my medical problems. A large lump developed under my left jaw. The dentist asked me if I was in the habit of picking a long straw from the field and to chew it, I said, "Yes." The dentist diagnosed that a parasite had entered through the hole in my tooth and was producing a sack of small grains, constantly increasing in numbers. The dentist operated to remove this growth, leaving only a small scar under my left jaw. The dentist said it was a very rare occurrence, and he would write a report to the medical journal.After leaving hospital, I was fit for training. I loved swimming in the sea. With a pass, I visited Tel-Aviv, Jerusalem, and Nazareth.

Stefan Maczka on Tel-Aviv Beach with Mochoń 1942

Travelling around Palestine I was surprised at Jewish achievements, modern towns and houses, orange and lemon orchards, vineyards, all watered by automatic sprinklers. In sharp contrast, the Palestine Arabs were living in conditions more appropriate to the time of Jesus Christ.

IRAQ

In early October 1942, my regiment was transferred by sea to Iraq, the main group travelled by land across Jordan. I was in the group sailing from Port Said to Basra, but due to a problem with our ship, we stopped in Aden for one week. The ship was regularly surrounded by small Arabian rowing boats; the young boys were excellent swimmers. We used to throw coins in the water; the boys would dive from their boats, (unless they were already in the water) and always managed to retrieve the coins. After a short stay in Basra, where it was extremely hot, we were transferred by lorries to be reunited with the rest of the regiment at Quizil Rabat. The 3rd Carpathian Division met the 5th Division in Iraq, which arrived in August from the Soviet Union. The two divisions were incorporated to form the 2nd Polish Corps. The newly formed 2nd Corps was now undergoing intensive training in Iraq. In our spare time we hunted for wild geese, deer, and wild boars, the meat had been used in our field kitchens. My regiment guarded oil installations and a petrol storage depot at Kirkuk. I remember the four hourly shifts; the worst was between 2-6am. Walking with a rifle around the 5 gallon petrol cans stacked up high, in total silence of the night, interrupted only now and again by the sudden noise made by petrol cans cooling down during colder night.

Mosul

In December, we were transferred to Mosul. We camped under canvas on the unused airport two miles from the city. I did not like this dirty old town, which was Out of Bounds to us anyway.

The only point of interest for me was the near-by remains of the biblical city of Nineveh, an old capital of Assyria. Entrance gates were guarded by two very large winged bulls, with human heads adorned with long curly hair, elaborately carved in granite.

The weather was mild, no frost and no snow, we received winter khaki uniforms, new 40mm Bofors anti-aircraft guns, Bedford gun carriers, Lorries, Bren guns, Tommy guns, revolvers etc. After being fully equipped and armed, we were subjected to intensive training in the cool winter weather. In our spare time, we hunted. Local Kurds were very friendly towards us.

Camp Monument Mosul.

Out of Bounds Street.

In February 1943, General Anders received a telegram from General Sikorski, informing him that Stalin has notified Polish Government in London on 16th January 1943 that all Polish citizens in the Soviet Union, originating from Polish territories now occupied by Soviets, are now regarded as Soviet Citizens. General Anders', Without Last Chapter, page 155, states: *13th April 1943, Germans broadcast discovery in Katyn of mass grave of Polish officers, laying face down in 12 layers, with hands tied at their backs in full Polish uniforms. Each officer was shot in the back of the head with a revolver.*

General Anders, during recruitment in Soviet Union was asking authorities what happened to 11,000 missing officers. He did not receive any satisfactory explanation. General Anders was now convinced that the German claim that Soviets have murdered those officers, is the truth. On the other hand, the Soviets were denying this crime by blaming Germans. In General Anders' book, Without Last Chapter, pages 160 - 161: *Polish Government in exile in London arranged for inspection of graves by the Swiss Red Cross, which clearly demonstrated that murders were carried out on Stalin's orders in 1940, well before the German invasion of Soviet Union in June 1941. Stalin, using this as a pretext, broke relations with the Polish Government in London.*

25th April, Soviets accused Polish Government of cooperating with Germans in anti Soviet propaganda.

Habbanyah

24th April 1943, my regiment was transferred to Habbanyah, just south of

Baghdad, and 304 miles south of Mosul. Our camp tents were setup in the middle of desert, on the banks of a large man-made lake, Habbanyah. We were issued with tropical uniforms, including cork helmets.

The temperature was very high, reaching 51c (over 120F). It was so hot, that it seemed like a hell on earth.

We were ordered to drink 10 pints of liquids each day, to ensure that we were sweating, which was the only way to keep the body temperature down. Lemonades and soda water were delivered by hydroplane landing on the lake.

After early breakfast, we were training until 11am. Then we were confined to our tents until 4pm. We were allowed out to latrines only while wearing a cork helmet. In the tents, we would fill our canvas camp beds with water and sit in it sweating profusely, reading or playing cards, mostly poker.

I soon realized that poker was a mug's game, so I concentrated on playing bridge. Now and again, we would point out to one person that stopped sweating, to have a drink. Without sweating, the body temperature would rise causing a heat stroke, which is very dangerous. Our sweating bodies were covered by white crystals of salt and fine particles of sand blown in by the wind. Almost every day, the wind would start blowing, causing a sand storm from midday until 3.30pm. We would emerge from the tents and try to clear the sand from all of our belongings. Next, we would run to the lake to cool down, the top twelve inches of water was hotter than body temperature. After swimming, we would wash our clothes, drying very quickly. Each day at 6 pm, we had a dinner. After dinner, we were lined up holding a mug of tea, the sergeant carrying a container of salt, would produce a teaspoonful of salt and bark an order: "Open your mouth, swallow the salt, wash down with tea." This was deemed to be necessary to replace the lost salt by sweating. In order to keep our drinks cold, we would wet woollen sock, put the bottle inside and hang it up outside the tent in the full sun. Normally by the time the sock dried, the drink would be cold. We were issued with canvas flasks holding one pint of water, exposed to the sun, the evaporating water would keep the liquid cool.

After dinner at 7.30pm, we would carry on training until 11pm. It was always too hot to sleep, so we would soak our mosquito net in water and try to go to sleep before the net dried, otherwise we had to repeat this operation again.

To our great shock and sorrow, we were notified that on 5th July 1943 General Sikorski the Prime Minister and Commander in Chief of Polish

Armed Forces, had been killed in a plane crash at Gibraltar, we knew that without him the future of Polish interests would suffer.

Return to Palestine

In August 1943, our regiment left Habbanyah, with all our equipment, for Palestine, travelling through the Iraqi desert in one continuous line, so as not to blow sand on the vehicle behind.

Descending winding roads into the Jordan valley, and to Palestine's cooler climate with lots of greenery, it seemed like being in Paradise. No more salt with our tea. We were stationed in El Khassa with five other artillery regiments. We had undergone an intensive training in British anti-aircraft training school at Naharyah.

Stefan Maczka (Third from the right) seated at the controls of the gun (Celowniczy) operating horizontal sight controls trying to shoot down the German plane. The other Celowniczy, operating the up and down controls.

We were now very well trained, and ready for battle. The discipline was strictly observed, emphasizing what we'd been told; *Orders must be obeyed, without questioning, why?* In our regiment, we had 9 batteries; each battery had to take a turn for a one weeks camp duties. Duties involved helping in the field kitchen, to peal potatoes and washing greasy kitchen utensils. The only way to remove grease was to rub with the desert sand. I hated those jobs. If I had a choice, I would rather dig a trench in the sand for camp latrines.

Each morning on parade, the sergeant would allocate duties, firstly by asking for volunteer. For example: "Who is good at handwriting? Step forward." Only to be handed a broom to sweep the compound.

After that experience, nobody would volunteer for anything, taking potluck on job allocated by the sergeant. Shortly after our arrival in Palestine, there was a mass desertion of 3,000 well-trained Jewish soldiers from the 2nd Polish Corp. Not because they were afraid to fight. Some joined kibbutzes, which had to be defended against attacks by Arabs; many joined the Hagan and Irgun terrorist organizations, including Corporal Begin (future Prime Minister of Israel), few joined a British Army. Out of 4,300 Jews, 1,300 had chosen to remain in the Polish Army as number of them felt more Polish than Jews; others didn't want to be deserters. In spite of pressure by the British, General Anders had forbidden searching for the deserters, declaring that, "Jews are fighting for their own freedom. I will not obstruct the fight which they have in front of them."

In his book, Gen Anders also acknowledged; *That British were right to be concerned about Jews joining the Polish Army.*

Gen Anders' book, Without Last Chapter, page 176. *In Poland lived 3,300,000 Jews, only 300,000 survived. Jews believe that out of 200,000 deported to Siberia 80% saved their lives from Nazi Holocaust.* In October 1943 I took exam Mała Matura (Comparable to to-days GCESE) with many other soldiers in Barbara, Palestine.

5th January 1943, my sister Danuta was transferred from Iraq to Palestine. Danuta was training to drive heavy vehicles. She was serving in the female Transport Company Nr. 316. I visited Danuta number of times in various places in Palestine.

Brother Ted with Danuta and her friend Irena Czarnecka.

Once I asked Danuta about her camp duties, she replied, "We have our own female cooks, but all the other jobs were done by the soldiers."

With Danuta and Irena Czarnecka in Palestine 1943

In 1943, Palestine, for the first time, I met my two first cousins. Left: Ted Zwolinski, Right: Edward Maczka.

Both were too young to join the army they were at Yunaks, juniors cadet school; I remember giving Ed 10 shillings out of my 15 shillings, 10 days army pay.

Preparations to fight Germans in Italy

On the 24th November, my regiment transferred from Palestine to an army camp named El Qassasin, 75 miles from Cairo. It was very hot in this Sahara desert; I had to wet mosquito net to be able to sleep and by 4am, I woke up cold, covering myself with a blanket.

We had to be careful of scorpions, tarantulas and black widows. We slept on the rubber ground sheet, with mosquito net tucked under the ground sheet, the boots and uniform within the mosquito net. In the morning, we had to shake carefully our clothes and boots, to remove any creepy crawlies.

12 December, the regiment travelled without equipment by rail to Suez, where we were issued with winter uniforms.

16th December, we boarded a Dutch ship, *Intra Poera* at Port Suez sailing through Suez Canal to Port Said, and across the Mediterranean Sea to fight in Italy.

We slept in hammocks suspended over long dining tables.

It was a very stormy crossing, and large numbers of soldiers were seasick.

Anti-aircraft artillery soldiers had to man the oerlikons (anti-aircraft guns) situated on the ship masts, I was one of the few who managed my shift without being seasick. With so many seasick, I could not find partners for a game of bridge.

CHAPTER SEVEN

ITALY: MONTE CASSINO

21st December 1943, our ship arrived at Taranto. We marched through the town to the transit camp, where we had to wait for our equipment from Egypt. Tents were erected on the damp ground. Compared to Egypt, it was very cold here. I remember clearly the Christmas Eve of 24th December 1943. I was walking alone through the empty streets of Taranto, watching Italian families preparing for Christmas. I missed my family, and felt really sad on that particular evening.

What is most amazing, that to this day I don't remember anything after that evening, until arrival in April 1944, at Monte Cassino. An amazing memory gap of almost four months.

I discovered from the Regimental records that from 4th February I took part in the battle at river Sangro, in the mountainous region of Campobasso covered by heavy snow.

Even after reading those records, and looking at the photographs of snow, how could I not remember this snow, so completely different from the Iraqi and Sahara deserts? But I still do not remember anything. It is as if I was not there at all.

During my talks about Deportation to Siberia, I never talked about that particular period of my life.

I only discovered this gap in my memory during writing this episode of my memoirs.

Battle at Monte Cassino

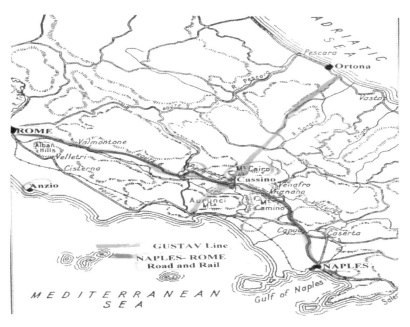

Monte Cassino Monastery was the most important point of Gustav line fortifications, stretching along the mountains from Adriatic coast to the Mediterranean Sea, completely controlling the road from Naples to Rome. The Germans also fortified the next defence line; seven miles back from Monte Cassino, named the Hitler Line, which included a little village, the San Germano in Piedimonte.

Germans had a plenty of time to fortify the Gustav Line.

The Monte Cassino Massif slopes, were covered by concealed concrete bunkers. Each bunker was protected by two other bunkers located 5-20 meters from one another. In addition, the slopes were mined and booby-trapped. Germans also used hand held flamethrowers.

In front of the above Massif runs a river: Rapido.

Germans were confident that Monte Cassino hill was impregnable and impossible to conquer.

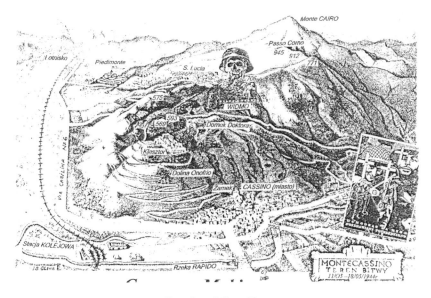

Aerial view of the Monte Cassino Massif.

From south west towards south east.

1944   Map of Monte Casino Monastery and Gustav Line

Hill 493   Hill 445   Hill 603

Monastery

tle Castle

'astello"   516   Hill 593

View of the Massif from west to the east.

The highest Mountain, 1689 meters named Monte Cairo on the right of Hill 603. The German troops overlooked Allied positions from Hill Monte Cairo 1689 meters, and from hills 706, 593and 569 on to the Monastery located on the hill 516.

Just below the Monastery hill 516, on hill 193 was the Little Castle. The Castello was an excellent Observation Point for the Germans.

Below in the valley, was the town of Monte Cassino.

To the left, was a Railway Station and road leading from Naples to Rome.

In front of the Monte Cassino Massif, runs the river Rapido.

From the top, Germans controlled the whole valley, including railroad links to Rome.

17thJanuary 1944, the first Battle at Monte Cassino started, mainly to divert German attention from proposed allied landing at Anzio.

American attack directly on Monastery Hill was repelled with great losses.

22nd January American and British troops landed at Anzio, 60 miles behind the Gustav Line. The Germans sealed off this bridgehead containing 70,000 American and British men.

15th February 1944 American planes bombed the above Monastery.

Two further attempts by Allies to take Monte Cassino Monastery Massif, were unsuccessful.

24thApril 1944, the Polish 2nd Corps numbering 50,000, now a part of British 8th Army, had replaced the 10th British Corps at Monte Cassino Massif. On Polish left wing, were British Commonwealth forces. Next, French, and next to them, the American Forces, a combined Allied front stretching for 20 miles up to the Tyrrhenian Sea.

German positions were defended by Hitler's elite crack 1st Parachute Division, previously hardened in the battle at the Soviet front. German troops were warned by Hitler that they must fight to death, as Poles don't take prisoners.

Polish 2nd Corps had to attack and take 4 main hills overlooking the Monastery, the main targets were Hill 593, and hill 569, which were the Gateway to the Monastery Hill.

I received a letter from Danuta informing me that from 4th of May, she will be in Italy with her Nr. 316 Transport Company, based not far from Monte Cassino.

She would be delivering supplies of petrol and ammunition from Bari, the main Allied supplies port on the Adriatic, to the second line of the front. On return journey, taking German prisoners to prison camps.

There were four female transport companies, including a canteen company, each with 326 Polish women drivers and personnel.

MY SISTER DANUTA
DRIVER 316 TRANSPORT

BRIEF SYNOPSIS OF THE BATTLE AT MONTE CASSINO

Currently, there are numerous books describing the above battle in great detail. First book was written by Melchior Wańkowicz, in 1946.

At the foothills of Monte Cassino, my regiment's anti-aircraft guns were protecting our artillery positions camouflaged in the olive groves.

During the night, German planes dropped bombs and leaflets on our positions.

Polish soldiers give up fight.

Surrender and return to Poland.

Our anti-aircraft guns did not fire on German planes dropping leaflets, mainly in order not to disclose our artillery positions. Allied planes dropped leaflets on German positions offering safe conduct to Germans, Italians and conscripted Polish soldiers serving in the German army.

SAFE CONDUCT

PASSIERSCHEIN
(wörtliche Uebersetzung des umstehenden Textes)

Der Soldat, der diesen Passierschein vorzeigt, benutzt ihn als Zeichen seines ehrlichen Willens, sich zu ergeben. Er ist zu entwaffnen. Er muss gut behandelt werden. Er hat Anspruch auf Verpflegung und, wenn nötig, ärztliche Behandlung. Er wird so bald wie möglich aus der Gefahrenzone entfernt.

GEZEICHNET
Oberster Alliierter Befehlshaber im Mittelmeerraum

SALVACONDOTTO
(Traduzione etterale del testo a tergo)

Il soldato che porta con se questo salvacondotto lo usa per dimostrare la sua sincera volontà di arrendersi. Bisogna disarmarlo, aver cura di lui, dargli da mangiare e prestargli, se necessario, assistenza medica. Al più presto possibile, egli deve essere allontanato dalla zona delle operazioni militari.

FIRMATO
Comandante Supremo delle Forze Alleate sul fronte Mediterraneo

PRZEPUSTKA
(Dokładne tłomaczenie tekstu na drugiej stronie)

Dla bojowych posterunków SPRZYMIERZONYCH ARMII: Żołnierz, okaziciel niniejszej przepustki, używa jej dla okazania swej szczerej woli do poddania się. Należy go rozbroić.

Powinien być dobrze traktowany. Przysługuje mu wyżywienie i w razie potrzeby opieka lekarska. Że strefy zagrożonej należy go bezzwłocznie usunąć.

PODPISANO
Naczelny Wódz Armii Sprzymierzonych na Froncie Śródziemnomorskim

General Anders knew that thousands of conscripted Poles served in the German Army. He believed that at first opportunity they would like to escape to join the Polish 2nd Corps. Trained soldiers will be needed to replenish the losses to be suffered in the forthcoming battle at Monte Cassino.

One of our guns firing at German positions.

Germans firing back at us

I fired my Anti- aircraft gun only few times on the German planes. We, the anti-aircraft guns crew, had to be ready at our guns at all times. Everybody else had orders to run for shelters.

The Germans fired at our artillery positions with wire wrapped around the nose of each shell creating a very loud screeching noise.

In reply, our artillerymen also wrapped wire on our shells.

After talking to the British soldiers whom we had replaced, we found that Germans did not use on them, the wire wrapped shells.

11th May, the Allies attacked on the whole 20-mile front. The battle was preceded by massed artillery fire of 1600 Allied guns firing on German positions.

The Polish 2nd Corps, had the hardest task to take the Monte Cassino Massif. Our guns, near me, fired continuously. The gun barrels had to be covered by wet blankets to stop the guns getting red hot.

Now and again, a bucket of water was thrown on the guns to keep the blankets wet.

The Polish 3rd Carpathian Division, during the night, in spite of suffering heavy casualties managed to capture Hill 593. In the morning light, they become clearly visible to Germans located on higher hills. German sharp shooters were killing our officers. Under very heavy fire, Poles were forced to withdraw to starting positions lower down the hill 593.

Nearby farmhouse, was used as an observation point and first aid station named Domek Doktora, the Doctors House.

Doctors house, Photo taken 2012 by K. Piotrowski. Below the above farmhouse were located two wells.

My friend, Jerzy Lis, the radio operator with the Observation Officer at the Doctors House, could not be relieved, until the next successful attack on hill 593 on 18th May 1944.

Mule Train

Mule Train Supplies and ammunition delivered only as far as mules could walk. Heavy casualties were suffered by mules and their handlers. When mules could not walk any higher, the supplies of ammunition and water had to be delivered on foot by the soldiers to the front line.

The only water available was in n the two wells located just below the Doctors house, pictured left. The water could be collected only during dark night in the bucket wrapped in a blanket, to prevent noise when touching the stone sides of the well. This noise would result in an immediate German gunfire.

17th May, the Allies attacked again on the whole front, Adriatic to Tyrrhenian Sea.

I watched our guns firing continuously, both sides firing non-stop at each other, the night almost turned into daylight. After fierce battle on 17th-18th May, the Polish 3rd Carpathian Division took Hill 593, and 569, which overlooked and protected the Monastery from Allied attack. At the same time, Allies managed to cross the river Rapido. As a result, Germans were forced to retreat from the Monastery, and raised the white flag. The white flag was replaced with a banner of 12th Podolski regiment.. At 11.15am, lieutenant Drabczyński, commander of the signals platoon of the 6 battalion, send a pigeon requesting a Polish flag. Pigeon arrived at HQ at 11.40am. The patrol from HQ arrived at the monastery at 2pm, with the Polish and Union Jack flags, followed by 40 reporters. Soon after that, the Polish flag was flying at the ruins of Monastery, joined by the British Union Jack.

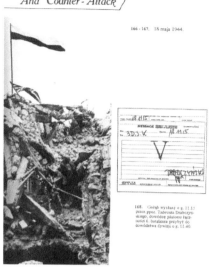

166 - 167.   18 maja 1944.

168.   Gołąb wysłany o g. 11.15
przez ppor. Tadeusza Drabczyń-
skiego, dowódcę plutonu łącz-
ności 6. batalionu przybył do
dowództwa dywizji o g. 11.40.

Please use magnifying glass to read small print (pigeon post).

Sergeant Emil Czech, (previous page), played Hejnal Marjacki 3 times a day, until we left for the Adriatic coast.

In the afternoon, the remaining two high hills overlooking the Monte Cassino were captured by Polish 5th Division, known as The Bisons.

The British 78th corps on the left wing from the Poles crossed River Rapido breaching the Gustav Line, pushing the Germans back to Hitler Line at San Germano Piedimonte.

Polish soldiers escorted German prisoners from the Monastery.

Polish soldiers strictly observed the Geneva Convention.

The Polish joy at Monte Cassino Victory was overshadowed by news of the Yalta Agreement between Roosevelt, Churchill and Stalin giving control over Poland to the Soviet Union.

We were very upset and despondent, no independence and no freedom for Poland. (We were fighting for a free Poland)

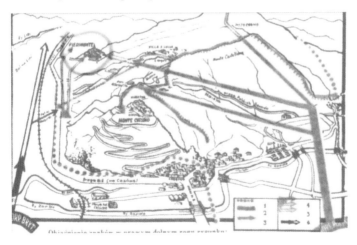

Battle Plan at Monte Cassino and Piedimonte at the Hitler Line. In the top left corner, the stronghold of San Germano Piedimonte.

With Gustav Line broken, our next objective was the Hitler Line at San Germano Piedimonte.

25th May 1944 after six days fight the Polish troops took Piedimonte, the last German stronghold on the Hitler Line. The road to Rome was now open. General Clarke the commander of the American 5th Army, joined up with two American and two British divisions now free at Anzio and raced for Rome. Instead of cutting off the German retreat from Gustav Line, his action prolonged the Italian campaign by one year.

As a result of this delay in Italy, 3 American and 4 French divisions were withdrawn from Italy to England, in preparation for the D. Day.

The Monuments and Cemeteries in Italy.

The Monument erected at San Germano Piedimonte next to the ruined castle in memory of the dead soldiers of the 6th Regiment of the Polish 3rd Carpathian Division.

The citizens of San Germano continue to invite veterans of the 3rd Carpathian Division to join them in the Annual Ceremony of Liberation on 25 May.

Recent aerial View of San Germano with white monument next to the building with the red roof just below the church.

The Iron Cross in memory of the death of the 5th Division on Hill 575

The Monument below, erected on Hill 593, in memory of all the soldiers of the 3rd Carpathian Division who died in the Battle for Monte Cassino, and are buried at the Monte Cassino Cemetery. All their names are inscribed on this monument.

Inscribed in Polish, English and Italian.

'FOR OUR FREEDOM AND YOURS, WE POLISH SOLDIERS HAVE GIVEN OUR SOUL TO GOD OUR BODY TO THE ITALIAN SOIL OUR HEARTS TO POLAND.'

Present aerial view of the 3DSK Monument on Hill 593

Polish Cemetery at the foot of the restored Monastery.

The entrance to the Polish cemetery at Monte Cassino is inscribed in large letters:

'Passer by please tell Poland, that we have died faithful in her service.'

General Anders the commander of all Polish Forces, General Duch, Commander of the 3rd Carpathian Division, and Bishop Gawlina, the Chaplain, are buried at this Cemetery, amongst 1,070 of their soldiers.

View from Hill 593 of the rebuilt Monastery in 1994, with the Cemetery just below the field of red poppies. 50th Anniversary in 1994 with Red Poppies in the foreground.

The song, *Red Poppies at Monte Cassino,* was written on the day of victory 18th May 1944. It became, alongside *Carpathian Brigade,* a second National

Anthem for the 3rd Carpathian Division, everybody stands up whenever either song is sung or played.

Polish Cemeteries in Italy, in addition to Monte Cassino.

Above: Casa Massima Cemetery.

450 graves of soldiers who died in the local Polish Army Hospital from wounds at Monte Cassino.

Above: Loreto, 1,100 Graves.

Above: British Commonwealth Cemetery, 4206 graves.

Above: Polish Cemetery 1406 graves at Bologna.

British Commonwealth Cemetery looking towards mountain.

GERMAN CEMETERY 20.002 graves

American cemetery is at Anzio: 7861 graves, listing 3095 as missing.

British Commonwealth cemetery at Anzio, 3078 graves.

Allied forces taking part in the battle at Monte Cassino, numbered 20 Divisions (about 280,000 men, including Polish forces of 50,000), against 15 German Divisions, keeping them away from the Soviet front. Allied losses at Monte Cassino were 22,000; Polish 1,520 including 450 who died from wounds at the hospital in Casa Massima. German losses at Monte Cassino were 20,052.

Polish infantry suffered heavy losses, which had to be made up by reducing the size of the anti-aircraft artillery regiment by 30%; three batteries 3rd, 6th and 9th were liquidated. Most of the men were transferred to the infantry. 3rd June 1944 I was transferred to the 2nd PAL the light artillery regiment. After the battle, we had a short rest in Campobasso area.

CHAPTER EIGHT

ADRIATIC CAMPAIGN

3rth of June 1944 I joined the 2nd Regiment of 25lbs light Artillery the (2nd PAL) as a gunner.

Shortly after I was called to the C.O. who said, "I got a job for you," pointing to a box on the floor, "It is a new anti-tank weapon called PIAT. You must learn how to use it, and to demonstrate it to our battery, instructions are in the box." I said, "Instructions are in a foreign language." The Officer replied, "You have Cenzus. (O Levels). "No excuses, find somebody who knows English, you only have four days to do it." I found one soldier who knew little English. Between us with great difficulty, I learned how to use this weapon and I gave a demonstration.

PIAT 3ft long, weight 32lbs Rocket weight 3lbs Range 110 yards.

From 5th to 14th June, the Polish 2nd Corps was transferred to Ortona and Pescara on the Adriatic coast to chase the retreating Germans.

The 2nd Polish corps front was along the Adriatic coast, up to Apennine Mountains, the British 8th Army was on the other side of the mountains, in central Italy, bordering with the American 5th Army, on the Tyrrhenian Sea.

Polish forces first objective was to capture Ancona, the main port on the

Adriatic. At first, Germans were falling back with little resistance, and then started defending at almost every river, blowing up bridges, placing mines. Our sappers were kept busy, building temporary bridges, laying steel netting for river crossings, clearing mines, repairing roads, and in the process suffering great number of casualties.

After brief instructions on how to use a field radio, I was sent twice to the front line with the artillery observer. I was radioing observation officer's instructions to our artillery position. I found this job sometimes dangerous but very interesting.

Battle for Ancona

After taking Loreto our troops were preparing to attack the hills overlooking Loreto, in order to take towns of Castelfidardo and Osimo, to open the way for Ancona, an important port on the Adriatic coast.

Early morning, 17th July 1944, I was sent as a radio operator to Loreto at the front line. I walked with another radio operator along the street of Loreto, to join our Observer Officer.

In preparation for our attack on the German positions, our planes, wave after wave, were dropping bombs, and our artillery was shelling heavily the German positions on the hill overlooking Loreto. Germans fired back ferociously, great number of shells flying safely above our heads. Suddenly, I heard a distinctive sound of approaching artillery shell; I knew from my frontline experience, that it would come down very close to us. Shouting, "Fall down." I lay on my tummy, steel helmet protecting my head, and radio pack protecting my back. I watched my friend running to the open door. The shell exploded just in front of me, shrapnel going up and sideways, then dropping down. Few small particles hit my radio pack and helmet, but I was not injured. I got up and shouted, "Are you all right?" No answer. I walked over to check up. To my horror, I saw him dead just in the doorway. He was hit by shrapnel in the head. If only he fell down beside me, he would have been alive. I will always remember this tragic incident. During our intensive training, we were told emphatically, "Obey orders and don't reason why." It was explained: "On battlefield, there may be no time for explanations, your life, and life of your comrades may depend on the quick obedience of an order."

Soon after this tragedy, I found my observation officer sitting on top of the tank. I joined him with my field radio, sitting behind the gun turret sheltering us from the German bullets.

In the background view of the Loreto Cathedral.

The tanks of the 6th Armoured Regiment (Dzieci Lwowskie) advanced slowly up the hill firing at German positions overlooking Loreto. Our infantry followed, sheltering behind our tanks from the German machine fire. Surrounded by all this noise I was radioing orders to our artillery to lay progressive artillery barrage in front of our tanks. But when our tank was firing, it was impossible to hear the radio and the observer officer.

That day we took Castel Fidardo and Osimo, forced the river Musone opening the way for Ancona. Our soldiers raided the accordion factory taking away most of the instruments. Our C.O. ordered return of all the accordions, except for few soldiers that could really play.

That night I slept on the riverbank in small personal tent erected over the dug out trench.

During the night, it rained heavily overflowing in to my trench. I woke up all wet. My pay book still has a water stains on it.

To assist 2nd Polish Corps on the Adriatic front we had assistance from 20,000 Italian army (Corpo Italiano di Liberazione) and partizans group, Maiella, under command of Polish officers, they fought bravely in conquering a small hill town Fillitrano just before Ancona.

18th July we took Ancona. It was a great victory for us, Germans suffered heavy losses in soldiers, arms and equipment.

We took 2,596 German prisoners, but we lost 34 officers and 2000 dead and wounded soldiers.

Next target were Pesaro and Rimini with Germans defending almost every river and canal, and as always blowing up bridges and laying mines.

Another turn of duty as Radio Operator

I would like to mention one more experience as a radio operator. The observation officer, Second Lieutenant Ilkow, took position on the third floor window of a hilltop house, conveniently overlooking German positions in the valley below. I sat in the scout car (an open top armoured vehicle) at radio controls, and radioed targets to our artillery position. The officer observed the first trial shot, shouted the correction target, which I passed on. Suddenly a fast German shot hit the edge of the window at which the officer Ilkow was standing. I was covered with small debris falling down, but no injury. Only when the dust and smoke cleared, I could see the officer at the enlarged window with another order, by then I opened the car door facing the building. On hearing a next shot coming, I dived quickly under the car. On returning to my radio, I could see debris and bigger bricks in the scout car. By the time the officer appeared at the next window, I was at the radio controls waiting for his order. I was not afraid, calmly feeling confident that as long as I could hear the shells coming, I could avoid them. As Lt Ilkow was not afraid of the shots directed at him, so I was also determined to continue with my duties.

Immediately after I radioed his order, I heard another shot. I dived under the car and was back on duty by the time the officer appeared at a different enlarged window. This time, he called out, "It is getting a bit dangerous; the Germans are firing at us point blank with the anti-tank guns. Let's go inside the building." The Germans obviously had a clear sight of us, so their shots were very accurate. Lt. Ilkow, on the other hand, couldn't silence the German guns with our artillery fire. I don't think he knew that I was diving under the scout-car before each shot hit the window. We met at ground floor, noticing a big hole in freshly bricked up doorway, exposing stairs going down. Stepping down, we entered a very large wine cellar, full of wine bottles, stored in brick built niches with dates on and labelled with details of wine. I picked up a bottle of red wine dated 1930. I noticed a lot of sediment, I said; "It's no good." And put it down.

We lost the telephone connection with our artillery, so the senior observer officer sent me to repair the line, which to my amazement was cut by artillery shells at every few yards.

After each repair, I would ring the observation point and the artillery position to check the line. Difficulty, was that there were many more cut telephone lines by the roadside; it was a problem finding the correct line to link up with the Artillery Unit. I was lucky to establish the connection before it turned dark. I returned to the observation point very tired. Next day, on return to my unit, the battery commander asked for my report. I told him that we discovered a big wine cellar full of old wine, which must have gone off. The officer said, "Get in the jeep and show me where the cellar is." We loaded a jeep full of wine to be enjoyed at the Officers Mess. On the way back he explained to me; "Old wines have sediment and should be handled carefully without disturbing sediment, preferably to be decanted." It shows how ignorant I was about wine.

6th June 1944 D Day landing in Normandy.

Polish 1st Armoured Division (originally based in Scotland) under the command of General Maczek in the first tank.

General Maczek generally commanded his troops from the leading tank.

29th July 1944, his 1st Armoured Division took part in the second stage of Normandy invasion, liberating northern France, Belgium and Holland. General Maczek, born 1892, died 11th July 1994, at the age of 102. In accordance with his wishes, he is buried with his soldiers at the Arnhem Cemetery.

Operation Market Garden in Holland

21st September 1944, the Polish First Independent Parachute Brigade dropped at Arnhem in support of the British 1st Airborne Division. Casualties were very heavy. British Division lost 6,986. Polish Brigade lost 411.

Warsaw Uprising

15th August- 5th October 1944.

Polish Underground Army helped Russians during their advance through Poland fighting the Germans, in return, received promise of help from the Red Amy. Polish Underground Home Army of 40,000 strong, attacked the Germans. The Red Army halted its advance to Warsaw at the banks of river Vistula. During 61 days of fighting, no help from the Soviets. The Polish 1st division (made up from Siberian prisoners) now part of the Red Army, tried to help the uprising, and on own initiative, established a bridgehead in Warsaw on the western side of river Vistula. After eight days without help from the Soviets, Polish division had to withdraw with 5,600 casualties. As a punishment by Soviets, the General Z. Berling was relieved from the command of the 1st Division. Russians refused landing and re-fuelling rights for the Allied planes to deliver supplies for the uprising.

Soviets were just waiting on the other side of the river, allowing Germans to defeat the uprising. Finally, in January 1945 the Red Army moved and liberated uninhabited 95% ruins of the City. During battle, and after surrender the Germans had treated wounded and surviving insurgents in accordance with the Geneva Convention. In contrast, the Soviets were deporting Home Army fighters to Siberia. Sixteen Polish political leaders invited under pretext of meeting, were arrested by NKVD. Stalin was determined to eliminate the patriots, in order to introduce a puppet government and communism in Poland. The German losses in Warsaw battle were 26,000. The insurgents 22,200, but Polish civilian losses were far greater.

Officers School of Artillery

29 September 1944, 1 was sent to the Officers School of Artillery in Matera, Southern Italy. For the first time since school days, I had to use Trigonometry and Logarithms. I remember on the firing range, we used the binoculars to calculate the distance and angle for the shot. Most of us made a number of corrections before hitting the target. The School Commandant, Colonel Ostrowski, would demonstrate how to fire just by looking through the knuckles of his hand; gave distance in yards, the degree angle, and his shot landed directly on target.

Distance between 1st and second knuckle equals 3 degrees, between 2nd and 3rd and 4th was 2 degrees between each of the last two knuckles.

Certificate of completion of the Officers School.

In front of the building photo of the initiator Kpr. Pchor. (Absolvent of the above school) now Prof. Dr. Wojciech Narębski

In 2005 The Commemorative plaque had been placed by the City of Matera on the above building, which housed the Officers School of Artillery during the war 1944 -1945. Written in Italian and Polish.

Stefan Mączka far right. The Sergeant 3rd from right.

With knowledge of school Latin and French, I quickly learned to speak Italian. After graduation 15 February 1945, I was seconded as Cadet Officer to the 3rd Carpathian Artillery Regiment, fighting for Bologna at River Senio, just above Faenza. This strong point was defended heavily all the winter by the Germans. My first duty was to take command of a gun crew comprising five men; I replaced the sergeant, in order to gain more gun firing experience.

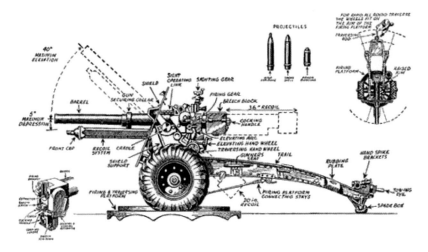

British 25-pounder Field Gun-Howitzer.

Rapid fire 8 rounds per minute. Prolonged fire 3 rounds per minute. Range max 12,500 yards.

I knew that my performance would be carefully observed. Unfortunately for me, the gun crew liked their drink; I had to deal with number of problems resulting from this.

The most serious incident, happened one night when our battery of four guns received an order to fire every 3 minutes on the designated target. I couldn't wake up my drunken crew, so I fired the gun by myself.

1. Open the gun breech.

2. Load the projectile (shell) in the gun barrel and then using the Ramming Rod, push it hard into the barrel. This is normally a two man operation. The Loader puts the shell into the barrel, and the Breech Operator, standing on the opposite side of the gun, rams it immediately, hard into the barrel.

3. Check, and if required, adjust the number of the explosive powder sachets in the cartridge, the number of sachets depends on the distance of the target.

4. Load the gun with the cartridge.

5. Close the gun breach.

6. Using appropriate mechanisms and instruments, set the gun barrel elevation and direction, according to the given data.

7. Fire the gun.

8. Eject the empty shell by opening the gun breech.

Start the same routine for the second and the subsequent shots.

I ran from one operation to the next. I was so pleased when after five shots the order came to stop firing.

Next morning, the battery commander said to me, "I couldn't see much activity at your gun position, but surprisingly the gun was fired at correct intervals." Then added with a little knowing smile, "Well done, Maczka." No mention was made about my gun crew.

In the next few days, I was transferred to the battery firing control. Targets received from Artillery Observer had to be plotted accurately on to the Firing Table, and double-checked using Logarithm Tables.

After a spell at firing table, I took my turn as an Observation Officer.

The Polish soldiers were very good and brave fighters.

I came across only one example of cowardice.

The cook in my battery unit always dug a deepest trench hole, into which he would dive in whenever we were fired on by the German Artillery, not coming out until firing stopped. So far, this always happened in between meal times. One day he dived in his deep hole just before finishing cooking the lunch and said, "I will not come out until firing stops." The Battery Commanding officer came, and ordered him to come out, then, pointing a gun at him, called out: "I order you to come out and get back to your cooking, or I will have to shoot you." The cook replied pleadingly; "Sorry officer, I can't help being afraid, shoot me if you must, but I promise that when firing stops, I will cook the lunch and I will be the best cook."

The officer just turned round and without a word walked away. Shortly after the firing stopped, the cook produced the meal, but continued to hide in the hole whenever firing resumed. To his credit, it must be said that he was a good and hard working cook. His contribution as cook was valuable.

Our target was to destroy the German artillery, and of course, they tried hard to destroy us.

The three Field Artillery regiments, and one anti-aircraft regiment of the 3rd Carpathian Division, lost 61 officers and 253 soldiers during the Italian Campaign.

Polish tanks entering Bologna.

21st April 1945 the Polish 2nd Corps liberated Bologna.

We were confined to our camp. No passes until mines around this City were cleared. My CO called me in and gave me The Tourist Guide to Bologna in Italian, and said, "I want you to give a talk about this historical city of Bologna, no excuses, I know that you can speak Italian."

This task was certainly easier than PIAT, it was not the first time that I was given unusual tasks to perform. I was wondering why my CO kept on picking on me with difficult jobs. This was not the first time my CO would say, "Nothing is impossible, if you really try. Nothing is impossible for an officer."

I visited Bologna many times; the city was very little damaged.

2nd May 1945 the German Army capitulated in Italy.

End of the war 7th May 1945

The end of the war was not a joyful occasion for Poland and for the Polish army. For Poland, it was just a victory over Germany. In fact, Poland lost the war and the freedom.

Poland now was totally under brutal and evil Soviet control.

In July 1945, the leaders of the above Great Three, decided on the future of Poland, without consultation with the Polish Government in London. Disregarding contribution to victory by the Polish Army, the 4th largest member of the Allied Forces.

Total Allied Forces at the end of War II were:

USA 11,362,000

USSR 14,904,000

British Commonwealth 5,456,000

Poland 594,000

According to the National Army Museum in London, Allied casualties in

Italy were 313,000. Total British and Commonwealth casualties were 148,000, of which 89,000 were British.

Polish casualties 4,070 dead.

The Allied forces in Italy tied up 25-30 German Divisions, which could have been used on the Russian front or to defend the Allied landing on the D Day.

Polish Casualties were the heaviest, (in proportion to the size of population). According to Polish records, the civilian losses were much greater than 5,675,000.

Total Polish population was reduced by 11,000,000. In addition to population losses, the materials losses were enormous, incalculable.

Encyclopedia Brittanica
World War II Csualties

Country	Killed, died of wounds, or in prison	Military wounded	Prisoniers or missing	Civilian deaths due to war	Estimated total deaths
Belgium	12,000	0	0	76,000	88,000
Brazil	943	4,222	0	0	1,000
Bulgaria	10,000	0	0	10,000	20,000
United Kingdom	264,443	277,077	213,919	92,673	357,000
Brit Commonwealth	108,929	197,970	37,805	0	109,000
Czechoslovakia	10,000	0	0	215,000	225,000
Denmark	1,800	0	0	2,000	4,000
Finland	82,000	50,000	0	2,000	84,000
France	213,324	400,000	0	350,000	563,000
Germany	3,500,000	5,000,000	3,400,000	780,000	4,200,000
Greece	88,300	0	0	325,000	413,000
Holland	7,900	2,860	0	200,000	208,000
Hungary	200,000	0	170,000	290,000	490,000
Italy	242,232	66,000	350,000	12,941	39,000
Japan	1,300,000	4,000,000	810,000	672,000	1,972,000
Norway	3,000	0	0	7,000	10,000
Poland	123,178	236,606	420,760	5,675,000	5,800,000
Philippines	27,000	0	0	91,000	118,000
Romania	300,000	0	100,000	200,000	500,000
USA	292,131	671,801	139,709	6,000	298,000
USSR	11,000,000	0	0	7,000,000	18,000,000
Yugoslavia	305,000	425,000	0	1,200,000	1,505,000
	18,092,180	11,331,536	5,642,193	17,206,614	35,004,000

Partition of Poland

Map of Poland after Partition.

Dark Blue Line Current Polish borders after 1945

Red Line: Previous Polish borders in 1939

Polish territory had been carved up; The Soviets took large part of the Eastern Poland up to Curzon Line, claiming that it was given to them in 1920 by Lord Curzon, even though they had not accepted the agreement at that time.

To recompense for the loss of eastern territories, Poland had been given German land, part of Prussia in the north, and land west of Poland. German people were expelled to Germany.

Soviets took north part of Prussia named Kaliningrad.

My father's land at Osada Krechowiecka was now part of the Soviet Union.

Poland lost 77,000 km sq of territory from 389,000 km sq in 1939, reducing its size to 312,000 km sq. currently.

Population reduced by 11 millions, from 35 millions in 1939, to 24 millions in 1945. Polish forces comprising 594,000 personnel, including Air Force and Navy, were the 4th largest fighting force on the Allied side.

(1st and 2nd Corps about 198,000, Polish Home Army, plus two divisions, which were part of the Red Army. Total 396,000).

CHAPTER NINE

AFTER THE WAR

In mid June 1945, my unit was transferred for a rest to Porto San Giorgio, a seaside resort on the Adriatic coast.

21st June 1945, I was seconded to the Divisional Artillery HQ, 3rd Carpathian Rifle Division Field Artillery Regiment.

12 July 1945, Transferred to the Anti-Mortar HQ, 3rd Carpathian Rifle Division.

1st September 1945, promoted to Corporal Cadet Officer.

I visited Bologna number of times with friends, by hitching rides on military lorries. We always stayed at Hotel Roma in the city centre, just off the Piazza Nettuno.

I remember one breakfast at the hotel, our friend, the Professor came down a little late, looking puzzled, and rubbing his cheek.

"What happened?" we asked, Professor replied; "I didn't do anything wrong, the chambermaid slapped me after I asked her where is the toilet." Knowing that his Italian was not very good, I asked him to repeat exactly how he said it in Italian. He said, "Dove a tuo letto," which in Italian means, where is your bed? "We are not surprised that she slapped you, asking for her bed first thing in the morning, when she is busy."

5th July 1945, Western Allies had officially withdrawn recognition of the Polish Government in London, on the same day, recognizing the Soviet sponsored Government in Warsaw.

This action produced despair, humiliation and anger for the 2nd Corps, but they were determined to support the Polish Government in exile, based in

London.

15th September 1945, Ernest Bevin, the Foreign secretary; issued circular to all Polish soldiers, inviting them to volunteer for repatriation to Poland.

The Polish Communist Regime, proclaimed that those not returning would be automatically deprived of the Polish Citizenship. Out of the total number of 207,000 Polish servicemen in Great Britain, 37,000 decided to return to Poland.

Those who returned, had not experienced life under Soviet Regime, and included:

1. Some serving in the Polish 1st Corps, based in Scotland.

2. Those who after the war, joined the 2nd Corps in Italy.

3. Deserters from the German Army. (Poles forcibly conscripted)

4. Poles liberated from the German labour camps, and few from the concentration camps.

But, from the original number of about 80,000 who left USSR with General Anders, only 310 soldiers returned to Poland.

Wedding of my sister Danuta

With my knowledge of Bologna, I helped Lt. Jurek (George) Gradosielski (engaged to my sister Danuta) to buy material for Danuta's wedding dress.

19th August 1945, 1 was at Danuta and Jurek's wedding in Porto San Giorgio. Lt. Jurek Gradosielski, VM, MC. served in sapper's regiment of the 5th Bisons Division.

I am in the middle of both photos.

EDUCATION

In October 1945, Danuta joined the Army Grammar School in Porto San Giorgio. 28th July 1945, I was seconded to the 3rd Carpathian Math/Physical Lyceum in Amandola, the little town of 4,000 inhabitants at the foot of snow covered Sibylline Mountains.

Amandola winter 1945-46

I shared quarters with two friends.

We were in the dining room of the first floor of private house at Via XX Septembre. Signor and Signora Accurti owned the house with daughter Rina. We made many Italian friends. We enjoyed our stay with the family, and lovely view of the mountains from the windows.

Antek Katowicz, S. Mączka, J. Kleinerman, T. Szymański

We had a busy schedule at school; we liked this town and its friendly inhabitants. In spare time, I visited Danuta at Porto San Giorgio. I also liked walking around Amandola enjoying the fantastic scenery. Christmas 1945, I visited Danuta and her husband Jurek. When I arrived, Jurek offered me a glass of drink, when I asked what it was, he replied, "White wine." I took a large gulp, and immediately started gasping for air, my brother-in-law started laughing, and said, "I should have told you that it was a pure spirit." I didn't enjoy his joke. In March 1946, we had a vacation between studies. We had a choice of organized eight-day excursions to Rome, Monte Cassino, or Lake Como. I choose a visit to Rome. I loved this ancient city, the Vatican, fountains, Colliseum and Forum. The streets were empty, without cars. (Retreating Germans apparently took all the vehicles), and pavements were crowded with pedestrians.

I received this photo from Danuta taken by Jurek during my visit.

London Victory Parade 8th June 1946

Poles, the fourth largest fighting force in the war, were excluded from London Victory parade in the interests of harmonious relations with the Soviet Union, and so as not to offend Stalin. All other countries were invited, even those that contributed very little to the war effort. British government invited only 25 Polish pilots, who refused to take part unless representatives of Polish army and navy were also invited. The British Army was greatly embarrassed by the absence of Poles, their brothers at arms. Lord Boothby, M.P. addressing the House of Commons about exclusion of Poles from Victory Parade, said, "We never lifted a finger to help the Poles." Since then, and up to date, and even after the Stalin's death, the Polish veterans continued to be excluded from the annual Victory Parades in London. There was one small exception, during Victory Parade in London, in 1995, with president Lech Walesa in attendance, ten Poles were allowed to join him on the stand, but no march past by Polish veterans was allowed. Polish Veterans Associations in Great Britain, decided as good British citizens, not to make an issue about this exclusion. We considered that we had nothing to celebrate; we lost our country, we only contributed to victory over Germany. We don't want to go where we are not wanted. Instead, we attended the liberation of Bologna parades in Italy, where we were always particularly well received. Since Poland regained independence, we started to attend Victory over Germany Parades, in Poland.

Transfer to England

Route of my travels:- Soviet Union , Middle East, Italian Campaign, England

In 1946, the Polish 2nd Corps who controlled the Adriatic sector until free elections in Italy had been transferred to England. 15th July 1946, my school left Amandola by train for Naples, stopping for few days in the nearby Lammie Transit Camp, before transfer by sea, from Naples to England.

My long journey from Poland, via Siberia, Middle East and Italy, at last is ending. I am looking forward to reunion with the rest of my family in a free Country of England. I wouldn't return to Poland and take a risk of ending up in Siberia again. Once is more than enough.

9th August, in Naples, I boarded Empress of Australia.

I was pleasantly surprised to meet Danuta on this ship.

Danuta was travelling with her school from Porto San Giorgio. Women and officers had cabins, the troops slept in hammocks suspended over long dining tables.

16th August, ship arrived at Liverpool.

Danuta with her school went to PRC camp in Foxley, Hereford.

My school travelled by train to an ex-American Airfield in Bodney, Norfolk.

All Poles on arrival, received a welcome brochure below. Translated into English by Stefan Maczka. (See following).

TO EVERY POLISH SOLDIER ARRIVING
TO Great Britain FOR DEMOBILIZATION
 Your arrival in G.B. is giving many Polish friends
In this country an opportunity to express again their wonder at the excellent armed achievements by the Polish Armed Forces, achieved on land, sea and in the air during last war. In one of hardest times of Polish History you were fighting bravely and without a moment of hesitation until the full victory over our common enemy. Welcoming you now on British Islands we wish to assure you, that we fully appreciate the debt we owe to Polish Soldiers, our first allies in the fight against Nazism, debt of gratitude.

Gt. Britain is facing many post war domestic difficulties, weighing heavily on condition of life for her people; it can't avoid affecting you. We don't doubt that with your contribution to rebuild this country you will display the same spirit of comradeship which you have shown to British soldiers your comrades at arms on battle fields. On our part we can assure you, that those Organizations, which we are representing, will use all efforts to give you help and make it easier for you to live in local communities. We believe that ties of respect and friendship based on jointly spilled blood, which was established between British societies and Polish soldiers, which came here in 1940 and in years following, will result in further strengthening after your arrival.

                JOINT   BRITISH   ORGANISATION
COMMITTEE
                FOR   WELCOMING   POLISH
SOLDIERS
London, 1946
66, Elizabeth Street, SW1

Polish Resettlement Corps (PRC)

Polish forces after arrival from Italy to UK, had three choices:

1. Return to Poland.

2. Emigrate to other countries.

3. Remain in England after joining PRC.

The Polish Forces in UK had to be demobilized. Most of soldiers in the Polish 2nd Corps had experienced Siberia, and would not go back to Poland. The soldiers remaining in England had to join PRC (Polish Resettlement Corps) and sign a two-year service contract. The PRC contract gave them right to army pay, accommodation, food, and to wear Polish uniforms. PRC retained military character under command of Polish Officers. The British Army was in control of PRC.

PRC soldiers were located in redundant military and air force camps, including former German P.O.W. camps. The two-year contract, allowed some soldiers to complete schools, and others to prepare for civilian life, and to find work.

In August 1946, Canadian Commission arrived to recruit 4.000 Polish soldiers for work in Canada. This offer was open only to the men without families.

Removal of citizenship.

27th September 1946 Polish puppet government in Warsaw, had taken Polish citizenship from General Anders, and from further 75 generals and senior officers in England. General Anders' book, Without last Chapter, page 385: *I believe on orders from Moscow.*

For this reason, some Polish Generals have requested to be buried after death, with their soldiers. Large number of officers and other ranks requested cremation, ashes to be taken to Poland, only after the country had regained its independence. General Anders, The Ex-Commander in Chief of Polish Forces, and Leader of the Polish Emigration, decorated by King George VI with an Order of the Bath, died 12th May 1970 in London at the age of 78.

His body was flown by the royal plane to Italy, for burial amongst his soldiers at the Polish Cemetery at Monte Cassino.

General Anders' grave at Monte Cassino Cemetery.

Later on, in this cemetery, were also buried: General Duch the commander of the 3rd Carpathian Division, and the 3DSK Chaplain, Bishop Józef Gawlina.

Left: Bishop Józef Gawlina. Right: General B. Duch.

School for Polish soldiers at Bodney, an ex-American Airfield in Norfolk.

Snow covered Camp in winter 1946/47

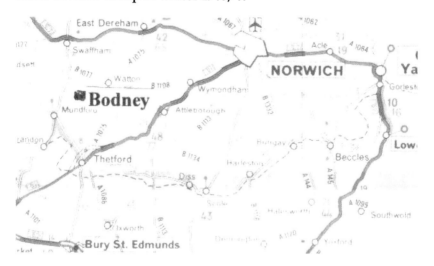

The Students were accommodated in corrugated Nissan huts.

The lessons started 3rd September 1946. After exams in December 1946, I obtained my School Leaving Certificate. The winter in England 1946/47 was very severe; there was no coal to heat our Nissen huts. The Forestry Commission allowed us to cut trees for fuel. I organized a group of tree cutters working under my instructions – my lumber jacking experience came useful – timber loaded onto lorries by the lumber jacking gang for transport to the camp, where timber had to be cut into smaller pieces for firewood. I spent the rest of the winter in the forest, providing timber to heat the camp.

Mr. Elliott (English teacher) and Mr. Alexander Gilson, the School Director cutting wood for fire.

My family and I had difficulties in learning English. We decided to apply for emigration to Argentina. I started to learn Spanish. With knowledge of Latin, French and Italian, it was much easier than learning English. In the meantime, more schools were transferred to our camp at Bodney, increasing numbers to 5,000 people. The sergeant major in charge of the Uniform Stores had found a civilian job. I was instructed take control of the stores, with assistance of two soldiers. I had to learn how to keep stores records, which came in useful later on. My father guarded German prisoners in Peebles, Scotland. He managed to bring Helena and Ted to Edinburgh, in 1943. I visited Helena in December 1947, reuniting with father, Helen and Ted for the first time since April 1942. I liked Edinburgh very much; I took part in celebrating the Scottish New Year in Princess Street, Edinburgh.

Above left: Helena. Centre: Father. Right: Ted.

May 1948, we had a gathering in Edinburgh, with Danuta and Jurek.

Next full family reunion, was at Penney, near Wrexham. Danuta was pregnant.

Ted, father, Helena Danuta and I.

Between1946-1949, 32,600 civilians, mostly soldiers families, and great number of orphans, had been brought to UK from East Africa, India, Persia, Palestine and Italy. Most of the soldiers in PRC had found jobs in coal-mining, building industry, textiles, agriculture and forestry. Those with education, enrolled to Polish University in London, and to various British Universities. I visited Norwich by bus many times, 30 miles from Bodney; mostly to dance at Mecca Dance Hall, called Samson and Hercules, whose statues were at the main entrance. I usually stayed the night at a small hotel opposite the Norwich Cathedral, for 10 shillings per night. (Converted to todays value = 50p), returning to my camp on Monday. I always wore a Polish uniform. I caused amusement at the ballroom whenever I asked a girl to dance. I clicked my heels and bowed. After a dance, I accompanied to her seat, clicked my heels and bowed, and departed to my seat. Some girls responded by smiling, and curtsying to me.

Returning from Norwich. I am second from the left.

My poor English caused a number of amusing and embarrassing situations. One evening, my dance partner said, "You can see me home." At a street corner, she said, "Goodnight." I said, "Where is your home," she replied, "Around the corner, good night." Really puzzled, I asked again. "Can I see your home?" She said, "No, good night." Only years later, when my English improved, I realized the meaning of this idiom. She only wanted to be escorted home, not to actually show me her house, as I wrongly assumed at the time.

In May 1948, The School Camp at Bodney was closing.

I delivered the Contents of the Uniform Store to the Central Army Supply Depot in Brentwood.

The remaining students/soldiers were transferred to the camp in Pipers Wood in Amersham, later on to the Camp in Horsham.

Most of the students managed to find a job, but my family and I continued to wait for the visa to Argentina.

July 1948, after transfer from Horsham to accommodation in Onslow Square, in London, I was given seven days to find a job. I received £15 in cash, demob suit, and National Registration Card to start my civilian life.

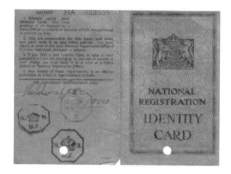

As an alien, I had to report each change of address to the Police.

I found a room in 5, Stanley Place, Victoria, rent 1.00 per week, and I got a job as a hotel porter at the Piccadilly Hotel, (Now called Le Meridien), next to Piccadilly Circus.

After passing bookkeeping exams, I started work as Wages Clerk at British Railways Stratford Works.

Two years later, after studying accountancy, I got a job at Treasurer Dept West Ham Borough Council.

In 1957, I started work as Accountant with Kind & Co. a small Building Contractors in Leytonstone.

After further studies and hard work, I was promoted to the position of Secretary/Financial Director of Kind & Co. Group.

In 1982, I reached a position of a Group Financial Director.

SB Maczka Secretary/Financial Director of the Garrett Group of companies in 1982

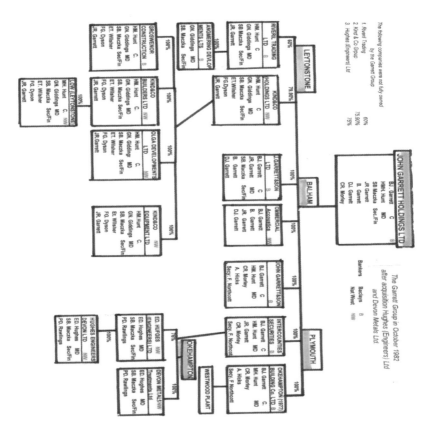

I Retired 30th April 1989

ITALY STAR
ASSOCIATION
1943-1945

SICILY
TARANTO . ANZIO . SALERNO
SANGRO . FOGGIA . ANCONA
CORIANO . FLORENCE . ORTONA
BOLOGNA . ARGENTA . PO VALLEY
CASSINO

NATIONAL CHAIRLADY.
Mrs Patricia White B.E.M.,
8 Buccobel House, Royal Oak Road,
Hackney, London. E8 1BT
Tel. 020 7249 1438

NATIONAL SECRETARY.
R.Quinton Esq., (102 Medium Regt., Pearl Yeomanry)
"Casa Laeta", 28 Boundary Road,
Carshalton, Surrey. SM5 3HG
Tel. 020 8241 0275. Fax. 020 8669 5520

NATIONAL TREASURER.
Miss M.D.Hanlon,
35 Ewell Park Way,
Ewell, Epsom, Surrey. KT17 2NW
Tel. 020 8393 5505

"When you walk in peaceful lanes so green – remember us – and think what might have been" We do remember them.

NATIONAL PRESIDENT.
Col. David E. Blum OBE (Queen's Royal Regiment)

NATIONAL VICE PRESIDENT.
M.C.Cheadle Esq.,(93rd. A/T Regt. 6th Argylls)

Continuation of précis by Roy Quinton of the Stefan Maczka story.

This, in point of fact, is not the end of the story of Stefan Maczka for, late in the 1980s, he had met a very charming lady, a widow of means in her own right, Evelyn Reynolds, whom Bob Smallpiece (Chairman of the Outer London South Branch of our Association) and I have come to know and very much respect. They are good company for each other in this last period of their lives. However, it is the end of the story as far as our readers are concerned.

Let me just say how much I respect this fine Polish Veteran and Comrade of the Italian Campaign a man who survived Siberia, fought the Nazis in Italy, and came to this country at the end of WW2 because he could not return to his own: was- "demobbed" with a new civilian suit, a National Insurance card and £15 cash in his pocket, with no job in view. But with the boundless determination (that seems to be the hallmark of all the Poles I know) to succeed and do well by his wife and children. He eventually retired in 1989 on a fixed annual occupational pension of £27,805 and a lump sum of £110,000.

Stefan has written:-"I started work with Kind & Co on a second hand bicycle and retired with an XJ6 Jaguar car."

What a success story!

Précis by Roy Quinton of an account contained in the letter of 19/5/08

Stefan Mączka delegate 3 DSK to Italy Star Association. Since 1992

THE AUTHOR

Stefan Maczka at age 90 (photo May 2013).

The President of the 3rd Carpathian Infantry Division Ex-Servicemen Association. Member of the Italy Star Association ISA since 1992.

Member of Leytonstone and Woodford Rotary Club since 1967.

My wife is English. I have 4 children, 7 grandchildren and 4 great-grandchildren.

Obituary.

Late Stefan Maczka. (Translated from Polish).

It is with deep regret to inform you that on 5 November 2014, Stefan Maczka died in Hadleigh, UK.

PA Capt. Stefan Boguslaw Maczka. Born December 31, 1922 Settlement Krechowiecki.

On 10 February 1940, he was arrested by the Soviets, and deported with his and other families of military settlers from Volhynia, to camps Kotlas in the Arkhangelsk region of Siberia. He escaped 14 November 1941.

In February 1942, he volunteered for the Polish Armed Forces in Guzar in Uzbekistan.

In 1942-1943, he served in Iran, Iraq, Palestine and Egypt.

In February 1944, he participated in the Italian campaign. He fought at Monte Cassino composed of 3rd Regiment of Artillery, 3rd Carpathian Rifle Division, 2nd Polish Corps.

In June 1944, he was a soldier in the 2nd Anti-aircraft Artillery Regiment, 3rd Carpathian Rifle Division, and a participant in the battle of Loreto, Ancona and Rimini.

In February 1945, he graduated from the School of Artillery in Matera, and then fought in the composition 3rd Carpathian Rifle Division in Faenza, Imola and Bologna.

Demobilized in December 1948.

After the war, he remained in exile in Britain. A dedicated worker for veterans, President of the Board.
Association Karpatczyków 3rd Carpathian Rifle Division.

Honoured with the Knight's Cross of the Order of the Rebirth of Polish Army Medal, Cross of Monte Cassino, Medal "Pro Patria" and many other honours, Polish and British.

In honour of his memory!

Jan Stanislaw Ciechanowski. Head of the Office for War Veterans and the Repressed.

POSTSCRIPT

Dad lived in England for sixty-six years, but Poland remained very much in his heart and soul.

A veteran Polish soldier, he remained loyal to the cause. Every year, he travelled to the sites of his former battles, maintaining and raising awareness of those who'd fought for their freedom and ours; lest we forget.

Philosophical about the adversities he'd faced, he was always so full of hope, and proud of his family.

He was an inspiration, and for all of us, his nearest and dearest, he will continue to be. To have had him in our lives for so long, was something truly magical. He is sorely missed.

To quote an extract from one of many condolence messages: 'The world has lost a great Pole.'

Close your eyes.

Think on him with pride.

A white-winged Polish eagle has taken to the skies.

Whisper goodbye. Goodbye Poland.

We'll see you again.

Sleep well, Dad.

Footnote:

I read amongst Dad's papers, a hauntingly, beautiful and heartfelt poem, *The Light of The Candle* by Hania Kaczanowska. Words have seldom moved me as much as this poem. Make a point of reading it for yourselves. Follow this shortened link to Google books: http://bit.ly/1yFqULu

Just beneath the poem, is the following message from Hania:

'Since the fall of Communism in Poland a new tradition has emerged.

On February 10 of each year, people all over the country place a lit candle in their window to commemorate the first four waves of deportations (in 1940) of approximately two million Polish citizens to Siberia.

I ask that you also light a candle in their memory and in the memory of all those who suffered through this Russian genocide of Polish people, and of the many other citizens of the Baltic countries.

A Candle Loses Nothing by Lighting Another Candle. Please keep this candle going.

Thank You.'

Hania Kaczanowska, 2007

From now on, I will light a candle on February 10, in memory of my father and all who suffered during that time. And I will tell the story to anyone who will listen.

Brian Maczka 1 December 2014

FURTHER READING

Too much to mention, but begin here, perhaps, and follow the trail...

Stalin's Ethnic Cleansing in Eastern Poland: Tales of the Deported, 1940 – 1946 Edited by Teresa Jeśmanowa.

Waiting to be heard: The Polish Christian Experience Under Nazi and Stalinist Oppression 1939 – 1955 Compiled and edited by Bogusia J. Wojciechowska.

Without Last Chapter by General Anders.

Visit the following website:

Virtual museum at http://kresy-siberia.org/muzeum/?lang=en

Printed in Great Britain
by Amazon

46533128R00091